A Perilous Profession

THE DANGEROUS LIVES OF DOCTORS

Kerry Breen

By the Author—

Good Medical Practice: Professionalism, Ethics and Law, 2016

Memoir of an accidental ethicist: On medical ethics, medical misconduct and challenges for the medical profession, 2018

A Passion for Justice: The Life and Times of Forensic Pathologist, Vernon Plueckhahn, 2019

The Man We Never Knew: Carl de Gruchy, Medical Pioneer, 2019

So You Want To Be a Doctor: A Guide For Prospective and Current Medical Students in Australia, 2020

Humanity in Medicine: The Life of Physician Dr Stanley Goulston, 2020

Ten Thousand Heart Operations: The Life of Cardio-Thoracic Surgeon Dr John Clarebrough, 2022

A Perilous Profession

THE DANGEROUS LIVES OF DOCTORS

Kerry Breen

Australian Scholarly

First published 2023 by
Australian Scholarly Publishing Pty Ltd
7 Lt Lothian St Nth, North Melbourne, Vic 3051
Tel: 03 9329 6963 / Fax: 03 9329 5452
enquiry@scholarly.info / www.scholarly.info

ISBN 978-1-923068-00-1

Cover design: Lucia Sankovic

Contents

Acknowledgements

A number of friends and colleagues, medical and non-medical, generously critiqued parts or all of drafts of this book and for that I am very grateful. They included Dr Frank Bowden, Dr Kym Jenkins, Dr Katrina Watson, Dr Bernadette Tobin, Dr Stephen Cordner, Ms Debbie Lee, Dr Daniel Tassone, and Dr Brendan Crotty. As some elements of this book may be contentious, I hasten to add that I take sole responsibility for its contents.

In addition, Dr Frank Shann, Dr Michael Wong and Dr Andrew Taylor kindly agreed to be interviewed regarding the life-threatening assault that each doctor survived. Rural GP, Dr David Iser, shared with me his insights into the lack of experience of medical students and young doctors in driving on country roads. A small number of doctors also discussed past health issues with me, including some experiences at the hands of the medical regulator. To protect their privacy I have not named them but they know of my gratitude. Medical colleagues, Dr Barbara Demediuk and Dr John Santamaria, provided me with valuable additional information.

As far as is possible, the material in this book is supported by published research and other published sources. While most of this information can be readily found in medical libraries or on line, there were some vital sources that were harder to locate. Fortunately, Ms Kathryn Rough, librarian to the Victorian Institute of Forensic Medicine came to my rescue on a number of occasions.

Last of all, I thank the publisher, Nick Walker, and his talented team at Australian Scholarly Publishing for their embrace of this book and for their dedication to publishing Australian works that the populist publishers are inclined to ignore.

Prologue

The impetus for writing this book came from the risks that doctors, nurses and other health-care professionals faced at the outbreak of the SARS-2 Covid-19 pandemic in 2020. Early in the evolution of an epidemic that was soon declared a pandemic, I read of an alarming number of doctors in Italy, over 150 eventually, who had died of Covid-19.[1] There was talk in Australia of bringing retired doctors like me back to supplement the medical work force. I wondered whether there might understandably be fearful doctors and nurses who would hesitate to accept their professional responsibilities to care for these patients. I wondered how the medical profession had responded to past pandemics. I wondered exactly how the Covid-19 virus was being spread. And I wondered what my response would be if I were to be called out of retirement. In the event, the Australian medical regulator chose only to offer doctors who had retired in the previous three years the opportunity to re-join the workforce, so I was saved a personal ethical decision.

But I was left thinking about the many risks that health-care workers face on a daily basis, risks that I believe young doctors rarely stop to consider, and risks of which the public are mostly unaware. I have written this account of these risks almost entirely from the perspective of a medical practitioner. However, I hasten to acknowledge that many of the risks described apply to a similar extent to all health professionals, especially to nurses in our hospitals and paramedics working in our ambulance services. I also acknowledge that members of other occupations such as our police forces and our armed services face truly life-threatening situations more frequently than do doctors. Most people would probably agree with that observation and thus those who seek to join those respected services will do so aware to some extent of the risks. However, I doubt that young people seeking to become doctors are aware of dangers that may lie ahead. Thus this book is written with the following intent: to inform the community of matters that are rarely aired about the safety and well-being of doctors; to inform prospective medical students of the risks that doctors are sometimes expected to face; and to explore what additional steps should be considered to reduce the dangers that doctors and other health-care workers face and to ensure their well-being. While not an element of my original intent, my research has led me to address what I perceive to be a significant gap in the ethical codes that guide the conduct of doctors in the face of these dangers.

In reviewing the potential dangers and stresses that doctors face it also became clearer that many of these have emerged or have worsened in the last four to five decades. With the exception of infectious diseases, the generation of doctors who taught me did not have to confront them. While the book does not attempt to trace this history in detail, in most chapters I have sought to provide some of this background. Hopefully these snippets of medical history will help to emphasise the extent of these changes.

There are some personal experiences that inform my writing that I should acknowledge. As I began writing this book I had cause to think back to two events during my clinical years that were potentially life-threatening. At the time, as most doctors would probably have done, I sought to minimise their significance. The first was a bout of acute hepatitis B in 1981 resulting from an accidental 'needle-stick' injury.[2] This occurred some years before preventive vaccination and effective treatments for hepatitis B became available and not long after there had been reports of the deaths from hepatitis B of staff working in the renal services of two British hospitals.[3] While I was unwell, obviously jaundiced, and off work for two months, I never felt that my life was in danger.

The second experience in around 1990 was more difficult to assess and it worried me considerably for some months. At the time I was the full-time director of a hospital department and had adopted the practice of having a sandwich lunch in my office on most days. On this particular day, the department secretary and the two other staff who occupied adjacent offices were out to lunch so I was notionally alone in the department. However, a male medical colleague had made a time to come to see me. We were seated in my office with the door closed but not locked when suddenly an agitated solidly built man burst into the room. His English was not good but it was soon clear that he was angry at the outcome of recent abdominal surgery and was looking for vengeance. While standing, he bared his abdomen to display not only his surgical scar but also a large knife in a sheath.

I am not a surgeon so he had found the wrong target. Because of the man's poor English it was not easy to explain this or to seek to calm him down. However after about ten minutes he agreed to leave. We later learned from carpenters renovating offices on the other side of our fourth-floor corridor that the man had entered via the fire escape stairs and had been lurking on the floor for a couple of hours. I concluded that he had waited until he could find me alone in my office and that it was only the chance presence of my colleague that surprised him and deflected him away from his intention to do harm. I was lucky but, as this book describes, many unlucky doctors have been assaulted and some killed by angry or disturbed patients.

While the risk of potentially fatal infectious diseases and of harm from violent patients are the most obvious dangers for doctors and other health-care workers, there are other dangers that can result in doctors being lost to the medical profession and even result in the loss of their lives. Doctors are at high risk of depression and suicide. Some suicides have been linked to the stress and shame of being the subject of allegations of unprofessional conduct or allegations of impairment due to illness, situations that may be aggravated by insensitive processes of medical regulators whose task it is to investigate such allegations. Some doctors are also at risk of harm from self-prescribing and self-administering addictive drugs. And from time to time, tired young doctors die in motor vehicle accidents after falling asleep at the wheel.

An overarching question that must arise is: are there reasonable steps that could have been taken or should be taken in the future to reduce the risk of harm and death, especially harm from violent patients, for doctors going about their work? Additional questions follow. Can doctors at risk of mental health problems be identified and helped before their health and fitness to practise suffers? Are there avoidable barriers to access to good care for unwell doctors? Are doctors' health services, designed to bypass such barriers, adequately resourced and readily accessible? Is mandatory reporting to the medical regulator by the treating doctors of doctors who may be unwell a help or a hindrance? Are there candidates for the medical profession who might be counselled to choose another career? Do the working hours and work load of junior doctors place them at risk of mental ill-health and of accidents – not only motor vehicle accidents but also needle-stick injuries and prescribing errors? In this book I address these issues and seek to provide answers to these questions.

As there are chapters in the book that address the health of medical students and doctors, I also need to declare an interest. I was deeply involved in the establishment of the Victorian Doctors' Health Program (VDHP) in 1999 and later served as the second chairman of its Board of Directors. The aims of the VDHP are to support and guide medical students and doctors whose stress, distress or illness is threatening their capacity to function. VDHP, which is generally regarded as a very valuable service, was initially funded entirely by all doctors in Victoria and is still mainly funded via the annual registration fees paid by doctors. With the introduction in 2010 of a new national scheme for the regulation of Australia's health professionals, VDHP experienced a serious threat to its existence. However, it has survived because several Victorian health ministers and the Victorian premier recognised its value at a time when the new national regulator for the health professions seemed inclined to let the service wither.

As I will describe, medical students and doctors who are unwell face many obstacles to accessing timely good quality health care. One of these obstacles is the legal requirement now placed on treating doctors to report unwell students and doctors to the national regulator. I will argue that such mandatory reporting is unwise and self-defeating as it causes delays in distressed doctors seeking help and thereby may expose their patients to risk. This and other badly designed aspects of the national regulatory scheme introduced in 2010 are in need of major change.

There are additional occupational hazards that apply to subgroups of doctors, including such things as exposure to radiation, noise, allergens, chemicals or gases, and injuries related to prolonged poor posture during some surgical procedures. However, these hazards are not the subject of this book.

In the book there are descriptions of how and why doctors can be reluctant to seek healthcare. I readily admit that I have been guilty of some of the unwise approaches taken by many doctors in this regard. Hopefully, if I were to begin again, I would follow the advice in this book!

One of the aims of this book is to inform prospective medical students of the dangers that they as doctors may face in clinical practice. In seeking to achieve this aim, I risk portraying only the downsides of being a doctor. People considering a career in medicine can be reassured that most doctors find their careers to be deeply rewarding, even if at times also demanding and stressful. I have written about these positive aspects elsewhere.[4]

1

A catalogue of the risks and dangers

Most doctors live out their professional years without suffering physical harm from patients. However, increasingly doctors are experiencing verbal abuse, threats of violence and actual physical aggression. In addition, putting aside the risk of injury or death occasioned by violent patients, there are other risks for doctors to consider, risks that may lead to outcomes that include the loss of the desire or confidence to practise medicine, the loss of the capacity and/or the loss of licence to practise, and more serious outcomes including the loss of good health or even one's life. These additional risks come via events that include exposure to infectious diseases that may lead to illness or death; burn-out, mental ill-health, depression and suicide; addiction to prescribed medications with all its consequences; and deaths in motor vehicle accidents when over-tired from work. Some of these risks may be magnified by denial and the related reluctance of doctors to seek professional assistance, as well as difficulties in accessing confidential, timely, and appropriate health care. In addition, the expectations of the community and other pressures now placed on doctors may be increasing the proportion of doctors in distress and in need of support.

Throughout history doctors have died from infectious diseases contracted from patients, most notably during the 14th to 17th centuries when epidemics of bubonic plague[1] recurred across Europe and other parts of Eurasia. The fatality rate from the plague varied among communities and across the decades but was claimed to be 80% in some cities during the initial European outbreaks from 1346 to 1353. It was even higher in the pneumonic form of the disease which was thought to be due to person to person spread.[2] Those doctors who were brave enough to remain at their posts had little or no protection from contracting the disease and presumably experienced similar fatality rates. In the plague epidemic that afflicted London in 1665, it was estimated that of the doctors who stayed to help, 50% died.[3] These risks to doctors created an ethical quandary for the medical profession then, and still do. While there were doctors who performed bravely during the plague, a significant proportion of the profession in that era placed their personal well-being ahead of the welfare of their patients and moved to live in safer rural areas.

The infectious disease of tuberculosis, known as 'consumption' until the causative bacterium was identified by Robert Koch in 1882, was also a serious risk to doctors before the discovery of the antibiotic, streptomycin. The discovery was first reported in 1944 and the antibiotic was shown to be effective in tuberculosis in a randomised controlled trial in 1948. Prior to the use of streptomycin, it was common for medical students and doctors to be diagnosed with pulmonary tuberculosis, contracted from patients, and then require months off study or work spent in sanatoriums awaiting spontaneous remission or death.[4] For example, the pioneer of cardiac surgery at the Alfred Hospital in Melbourne, Sir James Officer Brown (1897–1984), spent all of 1929 in isolation as a doctor while his lung infection cleared. At that time, the mortality from tuberculosis was high. The young doctor lived for the year in an 'open air' bungalow behind the home of a medical friend, isolated from all others.[5] Tuberculosis remains a major health problem across many parts of the world and can still be a problem in Australia in some communities and in people who are immune-suppressed. Doctors in Australia still become infected (see Chapter 6).

Influenza used to be a serious risk for health care workers and may be again in the future. There were assumed to be many deaths of doctors and nurses during the 1919–20 great influenza pandemic. The development of effective vaccines adjusted each year to meet the prevalent influenza strains, vaccines that are strongly urged on health care workers, have changed the impact of this disease. While influenza outbreaks will continue and deaths will occur,[6] at present the risk of dying falls predominantly on older people with underlying illnesses and not on health care workers. However, as discussed in Chapter 5, it is always possible that a new highly lethal strain of the influenza virus will emerge.

There will always be the risk of other lethal respiratory viral illnesses appearing, as was seen with the first severe acute respiratory syndrome (SARS 1) pandemic in 2003 and with the recent SARS 2 Covid-19 pandemic. Despite enormous technical advances in the identification of new viruses and in the capacity to rapidly produce vaccines, doctors and nurses at the forefront of caring for patients presenting with any new unknown illness will remain in danger, especially in the early phase of any outbreak. The deaths of over 150 doctors in Italy in the first phase of the Covid-19 pandemic should serve as a permanent reminder of this danger.

Fortunately, the SARS 1 pandemic which began in 2003 seemed to 'burn itself out'[7] relatively quickly but not before over 8000 people in six countries became ill, of whom 10% died.[8] Toronto in Canada became a locus of infection after two citizens flew home from Hong Kong with the virus. As a result 438 people were infected and 44 died. Over 100 health care workers became ill, three of whom died (two nurses and a doctor). For the staff in the hospitals of Toronto, the risk of returning home from work and infecting family members was so great that many chose not to go home between shifts.[9] All told over thirty health professionals (including 13 doctors) died of SARS 1 in the other countries affected by that pandemic (Hong Kong, China, Taiwan, Singapore and Vietnam).[10] Given Australia's proximity to these countries and the extensive movement of citizens between the countries, Australia was lucky to avoid the virus.[11]

In place of the long anticipated new deadly influenza pandemic, the world has recently experienced and is still living through the SARS 2 Covid-19 pandemic. In early 2023, the World Health Organisation estimated that nearly 7 million people have died[12] of Covid-19 while possibly up to 180,000 healthcare workers have also died.[13] As already mentioned, the pandemic has killed over 150 doctors in Italy and, in addition, 50 doctors in the United Kingdom have died.[14] In Australia, to my knowledge to date there have been no deaths of doctors or other healthcare workers, despite health-care workers being at three-fold risk of Covid infection.[15] The absence of mortality may reflect many factors including early closure of our borders, adequate access to (and appropriate use of) personal protective equipment for health-care staff, and perhaps less lethal strains of the virus reaching our shores.

In the last forty years, doctors in several sub-Saharan African countries have had to treat patients with the new and deadly viral disease known as Ebola or Ebola haemorrhagic fever. This is not a respiratory virus spread by coughing but is thought to enter the body via breaks in the skin or via the mucous membranes of the mouth, nose and eyes. This can happen from direct physical contact with a patient or a deceased patient or when a person comes into contact with the blood or secretions of a patient. To date, local outbreaks have been controlled by appropriate public health measures. The WHO estimated that between 1976 and 2012, there had been 24 outbreaks of Ebola resulting in 2,387 cases of whom 67% died. WHO has also estimated that ten percent of these deaths were in healthcare workers.[16]

Blood-borne viral illnesses are another group of infections that can be transmitted to doctors, nurses and other health-care workers. These illnesses include HIV/AIDS, hepatitis B and hepatitis C. For health-care workers, these viruses are a risk as the virus can be transmitted if a sharp instrument (venesection needle, surgical scalpel etc.) contaminated with infected blood penetrates the skin of the worker. This can happen during surgery or the taking of blood from a patient, or on the disposal of contaminated equipment whereby ancillary or nursing staff are infected. Transmission is especially a risk for surgeons operating in a confined space where direct vision of the surgeon's hands is restricted or when the surgery involves sharp bone spicules. These viruses have different degrees of infectiousness and different degrees of lethality; until effective anti-viral drugs were developed, AIDS was a universally fatal disease. In the first decade of the AIDS/HIV pandemic, because of fear of the illness, many doctors sought to avoid treating patients with HIV infection. The history of this era, the ethical debates that arose, and their gradual resolution, are discussed in Chapter 4.

Doctors are also at significant risk of mental ill-health, including burn-out, anxiety and depression, and suicide. Studies show that the suicide rates among doctors are higher than in the general population and higher than for other professions.[17] The data vary around the world but generally the suicide rate for male doctors is higher than the rate of most other professional groups while for female doctors this rate may be 4–6 times higher.[18] A 2013 survey of 14,000 Australian doctors and medical students found that one in ten junior doctors and one in five medical students reported having suicidal thoughts in the previous twelve months.[19]

Suicides have been linked to the intense pressures felt when doctors are under investigation over allegations of unprofessional conduct or of impairment through illness. In my view, the well-meaning efforts of medical regulators to be seen by the public to be proactive in protecting patients from harm has led to situations of doctors being declared 'guilty until proven innocent'.[20] This has been aggravated I believe by reactions to past scandals where regulators have failed to protect the public and by the handing over in 2010 of the regulation of the medical profession in Australia primarily to lay investigators. The balance between preserving the well-being of generally conscientious doctors versus the need to protect patients has probably moved too far in response towards the needs of the latter. In Chapter 14, I discuss what should be done to restore the balance.

As discussed in Chapters 7 to 9, the risks associated with ill-health in doctors are aggravated by factors that include denial, reluctance to seek help, and awareness of stigmatisation, as well as ready access to means of committing suicide. Medical students are also at risk of a similar range of mental ill-health issues. Governments in Australia (with the exception of Western Australia) have supported the national medical regulator in legislating for mandatory reporting by the treating doctor of any doctor who is unwell and thus may not be fit to continue to practise. In my view, in the view of many others, and in the view of the Western Australian parliament, the requirement that any treating doctor should be subject to this mandatory reporting provision is unwise and potentially harmful. It invites confusion between illness and 'impairment'. It is a requirement that almost certainly deters and delays unwell doctors from seeking help. For those who do finally seek help, the reporting requirement can undermine the trust that is need in the patient-doctor relationship. This legislated requirement seems to be peculiar to Australia as in most other countries any decision of a treating doctor to report when patients of an unwell doctor are at risk from the impairment of the unwell doctor is an ethical or professional obligation and not a legal one. In Chapter 11 I explain the subtle but important distinction between legal and ethical obligations and seek to address this matter in detail as it is a significant obstacle to progress and one on which health ministers and regulators obstinately refuse to bend.

Closely related to the issue of mental ill-health, and sometimes interwoven with mental ill-health, is the problem of misuse of drugs of dependence among doctors. Studies show that one percent of doctors become dependent on legal narcotics while up to ten percent misuse other prescription drugs. Some subsections of the medical profession are at increased risk. In addition, doctors can also create trouble for themselves through the use and misuse of illicit drugs such as cocaine and methamphetamines. And of course alcohol misuse is ever present; research indicates that this can be a problem for ten percent or more of doctors.

The most frightening of all dangers for doctors is the risk of being murdered by a patient. While this risk remains low in Australia, it is real and should never be trivialised or ignored. I have not been able to find a complete compilation of Australian doctors who have been seriously assaulted or murdered by patients or the relatives of patients but in Chapter 3 I recount the histories of six doctors who were murdered and three doctors who were seriously harmed by patients. In Italy, a recent study tabulated 21 murders over a 31-year period; in that study the doctors who died included psychiatrists, general practitioners and specialists. Some murders were committed by family members of the patient and not the patient themselves. Approximately half the perpetrators were deemed to be neither psychotic nor deluded.

It is even more difficult to determine how many doctors have died from falling asleep at the wheel of their car. Anecdotally this has occurred most often where young doctors, rostered to staff country hospitals, have driven home to their capital city after working long shifts, some after working overnight. Even if uncommon, such tragedies are preventable and every such event should be thoroughly examined and lessons learned.

Within the medical profession there has developed an increased awareness of many of these risks, accompanied by awareness of the issues of denial, reluctance to admit a need for help, and barriers to obtaining appropriate help. This increased awareness has led to a number of valuable initiatives including the establishment of doctors' health programs, peer support programs, and teaching of resilience. Unfortunately, as mentioned above, counterbalancing these moves to have doctors come forward in confidence to ask for help has been the introduction of mandatory reporting (including reporting by treating practitioners) of doctors' ill-health under the national regulatory scheme introduced in 2010. In my view, mandatory reporting by treating doctors is ill-advised, has negative consequences, and contributes to the lack of confidence that doctors have in the medical regulator, confidence that is necessary for effective regulation. I return to this matter in Chapter 11.

Australia, in common with many countries, has no central collection of data on the occupational health and safety of its healthcare workers. As commentators in the USA have remarked in regard to the health professions 'the number of deaths that results from occupationally acquired infection is an educated guess at best'.[21] In the final chapter, I recommend that attention be paid to this lack of data in Australia, along with the implementation of a range of preventive strategies.

2

The ethical principles underlying the duties of doctors

Some readers may opt to bypass this chapter because of its heading and their past experience of finding ethical discussions jargon-laden and obscure. I promise to avoid jargon unless totally inescapable for I too am antipathetic to the writing of many ethicists. In speaking or writing about medical ethics all one is doing is examining points of view and options and deciding under all the circumstances what is the correct or preferred path to follow or action to take. Beyond that, for most citizens, much ethical jargon is window-dressing.[1]

The issue of whether a doctor can avoid accepting certain clinical responsibilities[2] because they put the doctor at personal risk is central to this book. The topic has been little discussed in Australia. It seems to me that in some clinical situations this is such a troubling and threatening ethical issue that the medical profession has generally opted to remain silent on it, with occasional exceptions.[3] I suspect that this overall silence reflects the significance of the ethical principles involved, principles that medical leaders are reluctant to spell out and identify with, for fear that they themselves in certain situations would fail to meet the expectations and aspirations encompassed by those principles. However, I believe that the issue needs to be confronted and settled as it goes to the very core of what medicine and being a medical practitioner is all about.

So what do the international and Australian codes of medical ethics and codes of professional conduct have to say about treating a patient in a situation where the involvement places the doctor at personal risk? Actually they say very little. Apart from the UK General Medical Council's document *Good Medical Practice* which states '*You must not deny treatment to patients because their medical condition may put you at risk. If a patient poses a risk to your health or safety, you should take all available steps to minimise the risk before providing treatment or making other suitable alternative arrangements for providing treatment*' and apart from a recent update to the American Medical Association's guidance as discussed below, the codes say little of relevance (see Box 1 and 2). The ethical codes all emphasise the long-held principle that doctors must never abandon their existing patients without making firm arrangements for their ongoing care. But this ethical principle is negated to a degree by the claims that (a) no doctor is obliged to provide a form of treatment to which he or she is morally opposed[4] and (b) doctors are free to 'decline to enter into a therapeutic relationship where an alternative health care provider is available and the situation is not an emergency one'.[5] This latter statement, common to most codes of ethics, seems to have private medical practitioners in mind as it is doubtful that junior doctors employed in our public hospitals would be allowed this freedom.

It should be noted that the UK General Medical Council's document *Good Medical Practice* is a code of professional conduct and standards, not a code of ethics. There are distinguishing features between codes of ethics and codes of professional conduct that are rarely pointed out but they are relevant to this discussion. Codes of ethics deal with doctors' obligations at a high level and tend to be aspirational rather than directive. Codes of conduct and of professional standards (see Box 2) on the other hand are usually published as directives to the medical profession. In the case of the Medical Board of Australia's version of *Good Medical Practice*,[6] it is specifically stated that the code will be used '*to assist the Medical Board of Australia in its role of protecting the public, by setting and maintaining standards of medical practice against which a doctor's professional conduct can be evaluated. If your professional conduct varies significantly from this standard, you should be prepared to explain and justify your decisions and actions. Serious or repeated failure to meet these standards may have consequences for your medical registration.*'

Extracts from codes of ethics

The World Medical Association (WMA) International Code of Medical Ethics states '*The physician should provide help in medical emergencies, while considering the physician's own safety and competence, and the availability of other viable options for care*'. https://www.wma.net/policies-post/wma-international-code-of-medical-ethics/

The WMA Declaration of Geneva entitled The Physician's Pledge[7] begins with the words '*I solemnly pledge to dedicate my life to the service of humanity*' followed by '*The health and well-being of my patient will be my first consideration*' but says nothing about the situations discussed in this book. https://www.wma.net/policies-post/wma-declaration-of-geneva/

The Australian Medical Association's Code of Ethics states '*Recognise that you may decline to enter into a therapeutic relationship where an alternative health care provider is available and the situation is not an emergency one.*' https://www.ama.com.au/articles/code-ethics-2004-editorially-revised-2006-revised-2016/.

Extracts from codes of conduct

The Medical Board of Australia's guide entitled Good Medical Practice: a Code of Conduct for Doctors in Australia states '*Treating patients in emergencies requires doctors to consider a range of issues, in addition to the patient's best care. Good medical practice involves offering assistance in an emergency that takes account of your own safety, your skills, the availability of other options and the impact on any other patients under your care; and continuing to provide that assistance until your services are no longer required*'. https://www.medicalboard.gov.au/Codes-Guidelines-Policies/Code-of-conduct.aspx/.

The UK General Medical Council document Good Medical Practice states, '*You must offer help if emergencies arise in clinical settings or in the community, taking account of your own safety, your competence and the availability of other options for care*' and '*You must not deny treatment to patients because their medical condition may put you at*

> risk. *If a patient poses a risk to your health or safety, you should take all available steps to minimise the risk before providing treatment or making other suitable alternative arrangements for providing treatment*'
> https://www.gmc-uk.org/ethical-guidance/ethical-guidance-for-doctors/good-medical-practice/.

What does the law say about any obligation of doctors to treat? To my knowledge, there are no laws or legal precedent decisions that oblige a doctor to treat all comers. In actions for negligence, or with allegations of misconduct, where a person alleges that they were denied care in an emergency, the courts have relied on assessing any doctor's conduct by reference to the existing professional standards (i.e. codes of conduct). Two such cases in Australia went on appeal to higher courts and are worthy of attention.

The first case[8] in the New South Wales in 1996 involved a claim against a general practitioner who declined to attend a child suffering an epileptic seizure 300 metres away from the practitioner's surgery. Justice Badgery Parker's remarks at the first trial, viz. *'In general the common law does not impose a duty to assist a person in peril even where it is foreseeable that the consequence of a failure to assist will be the injury or death of the person imperilled'* were later adopted by the New South Wales Court of Appeal. The second case[9] was in Western Australia in 2013. Here a medical tribunal found a doctor guilty of unprofessional conduct for failing to render assistance at a motor vehicle accident but the decision was overturned by the Western Australia Supreme Court. The conclusions in both cases are consistent with the notion that any obligation to help in an emergency is derived from the medical profession's code of conduct and not from the common law.

In the absence of clear statements of principle in codes of ethics, national or international, how then do individual doctors deal with non-emergency clinical situations where by offering treatment to any patient, they might be placing themselves at risk of serious harm or illness? Do they stop to think about the matter? Is this something that is so ingrained in the training of young doctors that they know automatically that they must not flinch? Do doctors respond in accordance with their own values and their knowledge of community expectations? Are their decisions influenced by the existence of competing responsibilities, such as may exist for a doctor who, for example, is a single parent with young children to support? In the absence of ethical guidance, is there an historical tradition of exemplary conduct by doctors that might influence the behaviour of doctors now? Thus before seeking to answer some of the above questions, it is useful to look back in history as to how doctors have typically responded, especially in times of pandemics. The record of their responses is patchy. At times many individual doctors have responded heroically while some have simply fled to safety or fled the profession.

Some history

The ethical duty to treat has been widely discussed at various times in the past, most recently during the HIV/AIDS pandemic which began in the 1980s, and in relation to the first severe acute respiratory syndrome (SARS 1) pandemic of 2003. In these relatively modern times, the medical profession's reputation for being prepared to accept the risks involved in caring for patients with a potentially fatal infectious disease has overall been enhanced. Despite the absence of specific ethical or legal obligations to remain involved in the care of seriously ill patients, most doctors did not hesitate to take on such onerous responsibilities in patients with AIDS, with SARS 1, and in the 1919–20 influenza pandemic. This was not the case in earlier centuries as the records of the great European plague outbreaks in the 14th to 17th centuries[10] and an account of an epidemic of yellow fever in the USA in 1793[11] reveal.

During the Great Plague of London in 1665, when an estimated 15–20% of London's 400,000 citizens died, it is claimed that the majority of the members of the College of Physicians of London fled the city for the relative safety of the English countryside.[12] A similar efflux of doctors had taken place in many cities throughout Europe in the earlier outbreaks of plague in the previous two centuries.[13] Of the physicians, apothecaries and surgeons who remained in London in 1665 to care for the community, it is estimated that 50% died.[14] During any outbreak of plague, to provide medical care to poorer citizens who were unable to flee to the countryside, city officials offered financial incentives which were taken up mostly by younger doctors seeking to build their practices and enhance their professional status.[15] In an epidemic of deadly yellow fever in Philadelphia in the USA in 1793, the medical profession performed more admirably as it is believed that, with some notable exceptions, most remained at their posts and many died of the disease.[16]

Recalling that doctors in these earlier centuries had no knowledge of bacteria or viruses, no effective treatments, no protective equipment, and were dealing with new illnesses of unknown cause, one hesitates to condemn those doctors who abandoned not only their patients but, aware that the diseases were probably contagious, fled from crowded cities to safer places. Nevertheless abandoning patients was a common occurrence and led to long periods of loss of respect for the medical profession.

The traditional Hippocratic Oath is silent on what is expected of doctors facing a deadly infectious disease. Silent too is a USA version of the Oath as rewritten by Dr Louis Lasagna in 1964 and widely taken up by USA medical schools.[17] Thus there is a mixed historical record of the conduct of doctors faced with personal risk and little past ethical guidance from which the modern medical profession can draw its standards.

One exception to this absence of guidance was seen in the USA when the American Medical Association was formed in 1847 and the new organisation issued its first code of ethics. Perhaps sensitive to the reputational damage that flowed from some senior doctors abandoning their yellow fever patients just six decades earlier, the drafters of that first code included the following advice under the heading of '*The Duties of the Profession to the Public*' which in part read: '*...and when pestilence[18] prevails, it is the physician's duty to face the danger, and to continue their labors for the alleviation of suffering, even at jeopardy of their own lives*'.[19] This unique and clear statement endured for over a century, finally being omitted in 1957.

To my knowledge, no similar statement has since been issued in the USA[20] or in any other English-speaking nation.

There was a recent opportunity for the American Medical Association to reinstate this advice when in 2022 it issued detailed new ethical guidance for American doctors dealing with the Covid-19 pandemic. However, the Association chose a stance that seems to me to avoid the critical issue. Under the heading of '*Ethics guidance during a pandemic: An overview*', the Association updated its Code of Ethics with the following paragraphs:

> The duty to treat is foundational to the profession of medicine but is not absolute. The health care workforce is not an unlimited resource and must be preserved to ensure that care is available in the future. For their part, physicians have a responsibility to protect themselves, as well as a duty of solidarity to colleagues to share risks and burdens in a public health crisis. So too, health care institutions have responsibilities to support and protect health care professionals and to apportion the risks and benefits of providing care as equitably as possible.
>
> Many physicians owe competing duties of care as medical professionals and as individuals outside their professional roles. In a public health crisis, institutions should provide support to enable physicians to meet compelling personal obligations without undermining the fundamental obligation to patient welfare. In exceptional circumstances, when arrangements to allow the physician to honor both obligations are not feasible, it may be ethically acceptable for a physician to limit participating in care, provided that the institution has made available another mechanism for meeting patients' needs.
>
> Institutions should strive to be flexible in supporting physicians in efforts to address such conflicts. The more immediately relevant a physician's clinical expertise is to the urgent needs of the moment and the less that alternative care mechanisms are available, the stronger the professional obligation to provide care despite competing obligations.[21]

In my view, the very first sentence is open to more than one interpretation and its premise is disputable: on whose authority can the American Medical Association declare that '*The duty to treat is foundational to the profession of medicine but is <u>not absolute</u>*' (my underlining)? In addition, these long paragraphs do not represent ethical guidance but resemble more a menu from which doctors can pick and choose as each sees fit. I justify my views in the analysis below.

The Australian Medical Association similarly missed an opportunity to clearly state the responsibility of doctors in the face of a pandemic in its 2022 *Position Statement: Ethical Considerations for Medical Practitioners in Disaster Response in Australia*. The Association sat on the fence with these words '*While there is a general expectation within the community that doctors will accept a certain amount of personal risk when responding to a disaster, doctors are entitled to protect themselves from both physical and mental harm and should not be expected to exceed the bounds of reasonable personal risk*'.[22]

Weighing up the ethical arguments: ethical principles and related professional standards

At the heart of whether doctors are obliged to place themselves at personal risk lies a basic question: is medicine a profession or is it simply another commercial service? If any element of the answer to that question suggests that the practice of medicine is indeed just another commercial service, then the members of the medical profession of today will, in my view, be undermining the very concept of the original meaning of joining a profession. In addition they will be commencing a process of undoing the trust in the patient-doctor relationship built up over centuries, trust which is at the core of the practice of medicine.

To clearly explain my position it is essential that I first note that the words 'profession' and 'professional' are now so widely applied to so many different fields of endeavour as to become meaningless without further explication. Indeed, the Oxford Dictionary definition of profession simply reads: 'a paid occupation, especially one that involves prolonged training and a formal qualification'.

The Australian Council of Professions' definition comes closer to what it means to be a medical professional but as a generic definition it necessarily fails to capture many of the key elements of what the public truly expect of their doctors. The Council's definition reads: *'A profession is a disciplined group of individuals who adhere to ethical standards and who hold themselves out as, and are accepted by the public as possessing special knowledge and skills in a widely recognised body of learning derived from research, education and training at a high level, and who are prepared to apply this knowledge and exercise these skills in the interest of others. It is inherent in the definition of a profession that a code of ethics governs the activities of each profession. Such codes require behaviour and practice beyond the personal moral obligations of an individual. They define and demand high standards of behaviour in respect to the services provided to the public and in dealing with professional colleagues. Often these codes are enforced by the profession and are acknowledged and accepted by the community'.*[23]

What are the elements that are missing if one seeks to use this definition to cover medical practitioners? In my view, missing are all those qualities that underpin the trust that patients need to have in their doctors; some but not all of these elements form part of the Hippocratic Oath which dates back over 2000 years. The late Dr Edmund Pellegrino, a US physician and ethicist, eloquently explained the need for these elements in 2012 when he wrote: [24]

> *Medical care cannot be just a commodity. Medical care is a universal need which every person must at some time experience. The sick, whom we profess to treat, are vulnerable, anxious, and dependent. They become 'patients' when they decide that they cannot cope with their illness by themselves and are forced to seek our help. They are not 'consumers' of a product. Nor is that 'product' to be left to the vagaries of the marketplace. The availability, cost, and quality of health care are moral problems before they become economic problems. We have enormous power to help and to harm. We can easily take advantage*

of the patient. Despite this inequality of power, our patients have the same inherent humanity, dignity, and worth that we have. Patients are also in a diminished existential state. They are no longer free to go about their lives without hindrance. They feel alienated from the world of the healthy. They often feel guilty. Illness easily occupies the centre of their lives. This vulnerability means we must use our power primarily in the patient's interest – not the interest of the institution, the insurance company, the professional group or of our own personal pride.

I believe that to be able to deliver good medical care and meet the needs of their patients, doctors must exhibit (in addition to up-to-date clinical knowledge and adequate clinical skills, including good communication skills) the following key attributes:

Compassion
Empathy
Altruism and
Capacity to maintain confidentiality

Compassion has been well defined in a Canadian code of conduct as 'a deep awareness of the suffering of another, coupled with the wish to relieve it'.[25] Empathy in the context of medical practice represents 'the ability to understand the patient's situation from his or her perspective and communicate that understanding in a helpful (therapeutic) way'.[26] In our 2016 textbook, we defined altruism in clinical practice as 'a willingness to serve the needs of one's patients and the community even when this service might inconvenience the doctor or place the doctor at risk of disease'.[27]

On the topic of altruism, I am in firm agreement with Dr Pellegrino who in 1987, in the context of a debate over the duties of doctors during the HIV/AIDS epidemic, wrote: *'Nothing more exposes a physician's true ethics than the way he or she balances his or her own interests against those of the patient'.*[28] If Dr Pellegrino were alive today he would likely be perplexed and distressed by a recent definition provided by a Canadian provincial medical regulator which read *'Altruism, as a principle of action, is the highest commitment to service. Altruism in medicine is defined as practising unselfishly* *and with a regard for others. Patients' needs are paramount and must be considered before the individual physician's needs, the needs of physicians as a group, or the public as a whole. <u>This is not to say that physicians must sacrifice their health or other important aspects of their life for their patients</u>.* (my underlining*) Rather, it means that when providing care to a patient, a physician should always put that patient first'.*[29]

This definition certainly distresses me. I have reproduced it here to emphasise that values widely held by the medical profession and the virtues expected of its members are challenged from time to time and that the unspoken contract between the community and the medical profession on which trust in doctors is based should be closely watched from both sides of that contract.

It would be rare to find a serious commentator who would openly argue that the practice of medicine has been reduced to pure commerce. However, the conduct of a proportion of doctors, combined with, or responding to, changes in the way medical practices are owned and run, the almost total relaxation of the rules about advertising by doctors, and the advent via our media of 'celebrity' doctors, do at times create the impression that the profession might be headed that way.

In addition to the centrality and importance of trust in an effective and safe patient-doctor relationship and the need to always be aware that patients are generally in a vulnerable position, there is another aspect of the profession of medicine that separates it from most other professions. I refer to the long history of the means by which medical students and young doctors learn their profession; with the consent of society, students can study anatomy through the dissection of human corpses, and can enhance their knowledge and practise their required skills through the invitation to see and examine living patients. This has not come about by chance. It reflects long-standing acceptance by society that these liberties are necessary so that the society will be provided with competent, ethical and trustworthy doctors. The special nature of this agreement can never be overstated.[30]

Some commentators have expressed other views about the scope of the virtue of altruism and the degree to which doctors should be obliged to always place the interests of their patients ahead of any risk to their own well-being. The primary argument that has been raised has been one of informed consent; i.e. were doctors made fully aware of, or able to anticipate, what may lie ahead for them when they joined the profession? This was argued seriously in the face of the HIV/AIDS pandemic, when initially there was understandable fear amongst doctors and other health care workers (see Chapter 4). A secondary argument that was employed seemed to be that when situations change (e.g. the emergence of a new and frightening contagious disease) any social contract is open to renegotiation. The latter argument is seriously weakened by the absence of any mention of actual negotiation with the other party to the social contract, viz. the community. A third argument that is sometimes raised is that doctors are such a valuable resource that in order to ensure an adequate supply, they should not be obliged to practise in dangerous situations.

I do not place much weight on the lack of consent argument. After they enter the medical course, students and young doctors are extensively exposed to instruction about such matters as the need to be immunised against most diseases (not only for their own protection but to protect the patients with whom they come in contact) as well as the requirement to adhere to what are called 'universal' or 'standard' precautions[31] in undertaking a range of invasive procedures. Although young doctors may choose to put future risks well out of mind, I suggest that if asked, most would understand what they have agreed to take on in joining the medical profession.

My additional response to the informed consent argument is that it emphasises the need for the ethical expectations placed on doctors in the face of new epidemics of disease to be more clearly spelt out in the international and national codes of ethics.[32] That some doctors may not be able or willing to meet the ethical standards of the profession should not prevent the profession spelling out those standards. Indeed, the standards need to be there to clearly forewarn prospective medical students of the possible risks ahead. As mentioned, such codes have an aspirational element and it cannot be expected that every individual doctor, faced with new and uncertain risks, will be able to meet these aspirations. Nobody can be forced to remain in the medical profession and some clinicians might opt to change to a non-clinical career.

I am well aware that in seeking to meet this demanding interpretation of altruism, many ethical dilemmas will present themselves for doctors and for their employing institutions. For doctors, a very difficult decision may need to be faced in regard to obligations to one's family versus obligations to patients. For employing institutions and governments that fund them there will be the issue of seeking to make the work place as safe as possible, sometimes initially without all the necessary information or the required resources.

I need to add at this point my frustration with those writers who see codes of medical ethics as representing a form of a 'social contract' with the broader community. While I firmly agree with the concept, I am appalled at the almost universal lack of consultation with the very same 'broader community' with whom the so-called contract has been made. It is my belief that if genuinely consulted, the community would willingly support efforts (including the cost of those efforts) to help protect doctors, nurses and all health-care workers from the risks described in this book.

Finally in regard to the question as to how can the ethical obligation faced by doctors be best expressed in a code of ethics, here is my suggested wording: '*I enter the medical profession aware that in caring for patients there may be times that I will be expected to put the well-being of my patients ahead of my own health*'. It is clear that in the early months of the Covid-19 pandemic the medical profession met this currently unstated obligation willingly and bravely. This is evidenced by the distressingly large number of deaths from Covid-19 of doctors around the world.[33] This exemplary conduct is consistent with modern surveys of health-care professionals in Australia and elsewhere that indicate that the virtue of altruism remains strong.[34]

3

Doctors at risk of being assaulted or murdered

Aggressive behaviour and physical violence directed at staff in the health-care workplace are major issues throughout the world[1] and Australia is no exception. The incidence of violence is increasing.[2] It is estimated that the risk of doctors and nurses experiencing violence is sixteen times greater than that of the average worker and that health care workers are more likely to be attacked at work than prison guards and police officers.[3] In Victoria, in 2016, a report that combined data from hospitals and the ambulance service revealed that on average, every hour one staff member was threatened or assaulted and every day three staff members were injured.[4] It is not just in hospitals that verbal and physical aggression occurs as a 2011 survey of Australian general practitioners (GPs) revealed. The study reported that in the previous twelve months 58% of GPs had suffered verbal aggression, 6% physical aggression, 6% sexual harassment and 4% stalking.[5] A more recent (2022) survey of 378 general practices conducted by the NSW branch of the Australian Medical Association reported even more alarming figures: 83% of practices had experienced verbal aggression and 37% had experienced physical aggression from patients in the previous twelve months.

In hospital emergency departments around the world, physical threats and actual physical violence are so commonplace as to be regarded by doctors and nurses as simply part of their job. Consequently, under-reporting is usual. While the obvious sources of aggression are disturbed and unwell patients, instigators may be family members or accompanying friends. These emergency department health-care workers seem to appreciate that the behaviours they experience are often explained by the underlying health problem and/or the temporary effects of drugs (licit and illicit) and they are reluctant to pursue criminal charges. While such tolerance is admirable, there is also evidence that the same health-care workers can eventually suffer in terms of their own mental and physical health, leading to diminished enthusiasm for their work, loss of confidence and even medical errors.[6]

My impression is that frequent violence in Australian emergency departments is a relatively recent phenomenon. As a junior doctor working in an emergency department in the mid-1960s, such violence was almost unheard of. Furthermore, the employment of security staff in the emergency departments of our major hospitals dates back only three or so decades. Prior to that time, security was not an issue and access to these departments was unrestricted, so much so that in some hospitals the emergency department was a gathering place and communication hub for medical staff of the entire hospital. Now only staff with authorised passes can enter. Potential patients (unless transported by ambulance) face a security entrance where triage nurses and registration staff sit safely behind the same types of screens that one sees in our banks, designed to protect from armed robbers. In most large hospitals there is now a 24-hour presence of security staff usually co-located with the emergency department. It is also not yet adequately documented what has changed to render our hospital environments so hostile but the widespread use of illicit drugs (many of which – especially methamphetamine – are associated with unpredictable violent behaviour) is likely to be a key factor.[7] As Australia has one of the highest recorded usages of illicit drugs, it follows that the staff in our emergency departments are also at high risk of harm.[8]

As an Italian study[9] shows, and has been seen in Australia, violence or threats of violence can occur in any health care setting. This includes not only hospitals but also the private consulting rooms of doctors and psychologists, private homes when doctors or nurses visit, and for paramedics, in any work situation. In the USA doctors who provide abortion services are especially at risk. Younger healthcare workers generally may be at the greatest risk, possibly because of lack of training and lack of experience in de-escalation of threats of violence, as well as lack of awareness or alertness to the risks of any situation.

When a doctor or other health-care worker is seriously assaulted or murdered by a patient, the news sends a chill through the collective medical profession. For at least the next few days, most doctors will view each patient that they see in a new light. Although murders of doctors by patients are not common events, the risks are real. A recent Italian study analysed 21 deaths of doctors by homicide between 1988 and 2019.[10] Not all the murders were committed by patients as in six cases the murderers were relatives of patients. The sites of the murders included (in order of frequency) community clinics, the street, the doctor's home, the hospital and in one case, the patient's home. All deaths occurred during the course of the doctors' work. The deceased doctors included seven general practitioners, six psychiatrists and six surgeons. The authors assessed that in twelve of the twenty-one cases the murderer was not mentally ill. The most common motivation (fourteen cases) was revenge for various claimed harms. In six cases the revenge was preceded by stalking. The authors concluded by emphasising that '*doctors should be aware that the risk of being killed is not limited to hospital settings and that their patients' family members might also pose a threat to them*'.[11] As we will see below, the homicides of Australian doctors show similar characteristics.

There has been no similar systematic study of the work-related homicide of doctors in Australia and my search for instances in preparing for this book is undoubtedly incomplete. One media report in 2008[12] quoted a doctor who, distressed by a recent tragic death of a Melbourne general practitioner, spoke of her knowledge of at least seven murders of Australian doctors in the previous decade. I have not been able to confirm that figure. The same doctor called for a national register of assaults against doctors. The Federal health minister was said to be prepared to examine any such proposal but nothing has ever emerged.[13]

All instances of homicide of doctors in the course of their duties are tragedies so it would be insensitive to declare any instance more tragic than others. However, the death of Australian psychiatrist Dr Margaret Tobin in Adelaide in 2002 was clearly so.[14] Dr Tobin, whose family emigrated from Ireland when she was very young, graduated from the University of Melbourne in 1978. She trained to become a psychiatrist and it was not long before it became clear that she had a passion to improve the provision of mental health services in Australia and the administrative capacity to achieve this. She led improvements in standards of care in a number of Victorian mental health hospitals and in 1993 was recruited to a leadership role at St George's Hospital in Sydney where she also served as the director of mental health for the Southern Sydney Area Health Service. One of the staff psychiatrists reporting to her at St George's was a Dr Eric Gassy, a University of Sydney graduate, also an immigrant as a child, in his case from Mauritius.

Prior to Dr Tobin's arrival at St George's, Dr Gassy had been appointed as acting head of psychiatry. Soon after Dr Tobin took up her appointment, Dr Gassy went on extended sick leave for what one medical certificate said was 'burn-out'. Dr Gassy's doctor provided medical certificates but Gassy denied that that doctor was treating him. In addition, Dr Tobin became aware of complaints from staff that raised the possibility that Gassy was mentally unwell as there were reports of paranoid tendencies, conflict with staff, and alleged inappropriate approaches to female staff members.

Dr Gassy was keen to return to work but refused to provide Dr Tobin with a treating doctor's report to testify that he was sufficiently well enough to treat patients. In view of this refusal, and wanting Dr Gassy's fitness to practise assessed, Dr Tobin notified the Medical Board of New South Wales of these concerns, requesting an independent assessment. Such notifications are common responsibilities of medical administrators. Even had Dr Tobin anticipated the possible consequences, her first duty was to protect other patients and her ethical concerns are likely to have always taken precedence.

In 1994, the NSW Medical Board's appointed psychiatrist diagnosed Gassy with a paranoid and delusional state. He advised the need for treatment but predicted that Dr Gassy would not accept this advice. Meanwhile Dr Gassy was secretly seeking a medical opinion from a trainee psychiatrist who he knew. The opinion of that inexperienced doctor unfortunately reinforced Gassy's view that he was not unwell and that Dr Tobin, by involving the Medical Board, was biased against him.

On the basis of the independent psychiatrist's report, Dr Gassy appeared before the Board's Impaired Registrant's Panel. The Panel sought to direct Dr Gassy into psychiatric care which he rejected. The Medical Board then placed conditions on Dr Gassy's registration, conditions that he refused to accept, still claiming that he was not mentally unwell. This stand-off continued for another two years during which time Dr Gassy was not working as a doctor. Eventually the Board brought matters to a head by referring him to the NSW Medical Tribunal on the grounds that his refusal to accept conditions on his registration represented unprofessional conduct. That Tribunal hearing was held in 1997 and resulted in the removal of Dr Gassy's name from the medical register. The Chair of the Tribunal made it clear that should Dr Gassy change his mind and accept the condition of seeing a Board-appointed psychiatrist, an application for restoration to the register would be looked on favourably. However the Medical Board heard no more from him. From that point, Gassy kept a low profile and did not draw attention to himself for another five years.

In the meanwhile, Dr Tobin moved to Adelaide where she took on a more senior role as director of mental health services for the state of South Australia. In this role, she occupied an office on the eighth floor of the Health Department building in central Adelaide. On Monday 14 October 2002, she returned from a quick lunch and entered a lift with two colleagues and another man who was unknown to her or her colleagues. The two colleagues got out of the lift on the seventh floor. Dr Tobin exited on the eighth floor and turned towards her office. She was then shot four times in the back at close range. She never saw the gunman. Ambulance help came promptly but she died shortly after arrival at the Royal Adelaide Hospital.

The shooting caused great alarm within the Health Department building and the surrounding business district as initially it was feared that the gunman was still in the area and that the first killing was the start of a larger vendetta or even a terrorist attack.[15] The police initially had few leads as nobody was able to provide a description of the gunman. The staff who rushed to Dr Tobin's aid had not seen the gunman and were unaware how he had escaped the scene. Assuming that the gunman was the man in the lift with Dr Tobin, the police created an identikit image based on her colleagues' recall of a man with long dark hair and a dark beard.

The identikit image gave the South Australian police the breakthrough they needed. Staff from a Brisbane conference venue made contact, reporting that they had seen a bearded man behaving suspiciously at a conference of psychiatrists held in Brisbane six months earlier. When challenged, the man left the building quickly, briefly dropping something that sounded metallic like a gun. Those observers thought that the man's appearance bore some resemblance to the identikit image that the police had circulated. As Dr Tobin had attended that conference as a keynote speaker, the police now considered the possibility that Dr Tobin was being stalked. Thus the police looked back for any person who might bear a grudge against her and this brought into their sights unregistered Dr Gassy who was still living in Sydney.

Via exemplary detective work, the police also found security camera footage of a man who fitted their identikit image dumping a plastic bag in a waste bin at a petrol station in Renmark, on the route from Adelaide to Sydney. They retrieved the bag from the local rubbish tip and found receipts for motels located between Sydney and Adelaide and for motels located between Sydney and Brisbane. The bag also contained a discarded jacket that showed traces of gunpowder. Before approaching Gassy, the police were able to find evidence that he had rented cars under a false name at the time of the Adelaide shooting and at the time of the earlier possible sighting in Brisbane. They also established that the odometer readings on the rented cars were consistent with such long travel. Later they obtained evidence from the receptionist at the Adelaide motel where, again using a false name, Dr Gassy had stayed for one night before the shooting. The receptionist recalled that the bearded man who had checked in appeared scruffy and unkempt. The next day, he had asked her where he could get a haircut. When he returned, she was astounded at his change of appearance as his beard had gone.

When the police obtained a search warrant and raided Dr Gassy's house in Sydney, they found a list of names of several of the doctors who had been party to the NSW Medical Board's task of assessing his mental health. Dr Tobin's name was not on the list but the list had been torn leaving behind just the letter 'M'. From further interviews with motel staff, the police were confident that Gassy had driven from Sydney to Adelaide, almost certainly with the sole intent of murdering Dr Tobin. In addition, the police had evidence that Gassy had purchased two deadly Glock pistols and had trained as a marksman and in counter-surveillance.

The police and the public prosecutor determined that, while all their evidence was circumstantial and while Gassy denied that he was the killer, the case should go to trial. The trial lasted eleven weeks and the jury heard evidence from 163 witnesses. Gassy was found guilty of murder but successfully appealed to the High Court on the grounds that some directions given to the jury by the presiding judge were unbalanced. At a retrial, the new jury found him guilty and he was sentenced to life imprisonment, with a 34-year non-parole period.

If you as a reader think that this is all there is to this sad story, then stop for a moment to consider the impact of this murder not only on Dr Tobin's family but also on other doctors. We do not know the names of all the other people who were on Gassy's hit list but the publicly available reports of the NSW Medical Tribunal, and the reports of the trial, the two appeals, including one to the High Court, and the second trial give us some idea. In addition, one of his targets has 'outed' himself,[16] thereby providing an insight into the enormous stress that several senior doctors and their families endured, until Gassy was apprehended, for simply doing their duty for the community. Life sentence in South Australia, as in most other Australian jurisdictions, is not truly for life. In 2009 Gassy successfully applied for an earlier potential parole date, now reduced to 30 years. Thus former doctor Eric Gassy could be released as early as 2034. He will be 78 years of age with his paranoid and delusional state probably untreated. At least two of his original doctor targets may then still be alive.

For every doctor who has been murdered by a patient, there are at least as many who have been very seriously harmed and who came close to dying. The following story of a Victorian general practitioner, Dr Andrew Taylor, who luckily survived five bullet wounds, is one of remarkable courage and quick thinking on the part of the doctor.[17] However, the medical history of the patient who shot him is so commonplace that it should alarm every doctor and make all alert to steps that could be taken ensure greater safety (as will be discussed in Chapter 14). The story also emphasises the collateral harm that can be associated with brutal assaults in the work place.

The shooting took place in April 1997 at Hastings, a small town on Victoria's Mornington Peninsula. In this case, the task of the police was much simpler than it was in the case of Dr Gassy. The assailant was still at the scene when the police arrived as he had shot himself once in the chest after the attack. He was a middle-aged man who had migrated from central Europe at the age of 22 years. Of below average intelligence, his employment record was primarily one of physical work. In 1982 he suffered a back injury from a fall at work. He sought workers' compensation, eventually being awarded $30,000 in 1986. In the intervening four years he had received sickness benefits and then an invalid pension. In 1987 the pension was cancelled and he was supported by unemployment benefits. He struggled to find work. In 1989 he was a passenger in a car accident where two other occupants of the car died. He suffered a broken pelvis, broken ribs, a punctured lung and a broken jaw, and was in hospital for three months.

Following the car accident there were drawn out legal proceedings with the Victorian Transport Accident Commission over his claim for his injuries, proceedings that were only settled seven years later. In those seven years, he attended the Hastings general practice over 100 times. During those years, he experienced increasing depression and anger and at times exhibited a degree of paranoia towards his lawyers. He had anticipated a damages award of over a million dollars but received only $350,000. He blamed the low sum on the medical reports of his general practitioners.

Following this news, he first sought to confront his usual GP at the

GP's home but the doctor was away. That same morning, a Saturday, he attended the GP practice not knowing which doctor would be present. The Saturday clinic was for urgent cases only and the clinic was staffed by a receptionist and Dr Taylor. Here he was welcomed by the receptionist and by Dr Taylor who came into the reception area to meet him. In an adjacent waiting room were other patients including at least one child.

In front of the receptionist, the man drew a gun and, telling Dr Taylor that now he would understand the suffering that the patient had experienced, shot him in the left leg, the upper right leg and the buttock. As Dr Taylor tried to crawl to safety, he was shot twice more in the back. While the attacker was reloading his gun, Dr Taylor pleaded for permission to call his family, telling the man that 'you have killed me, at least let me call my family to say goodbye'. The man replied 'No, I haven't killed you but I will kill myself. You'll remember me through all these injuries, and you will understand all the pain I have gone through'. The man then shot himself once in the chest. Dr Taylor and his attacker were air-lifted by helicopter to the Alfred Hospital in Melbourne. Both survived. Dr Taylor needed multiple operations and was off work for nine months.

When the matter came before the Victorian Supreme Court in 1999, the attacker pleaded guilty to a charge of intentionally causing serious injury to Dr Taylor and expressed remorse. Psychiatric assessments excluded a paranoid psychosis and instead emphasised his severe depression, anger and poor coping skills to partly explain the assault. He was sentenced to six years imprisonment with a minimum of four years before being eligible for parole.

In the sentencing report, the judge noted the distress experienced by the receptionist and the long time that it took for her to recover. We have no record of the experiences of the patients in the waiting room (adults and child) but it takes little imagination to appreciate that they too must have been traumatised.

As in the Italian study, the motive for physical assault, attempted murder and murder in Australia (in sites other than the emergency department) is usually revenge: revenge for such things as a poor surgical outcome, death of a relative, failure to achieve adequate compensation for workplace and other injuries, or some type of real or perceived slight. In some instances, attacks have been random and linked to severe psychosis suffered by the assailant. There has been no Australian study equivalent to the Italian study of murdered doctors. This chapter does not claim to list all those Australian doctors who have been murdered in relation to their professional duties. The following additional instances have been chosen to exemplify how random and unpredictable such attacks can be. In the first of the cases, the doctor was lucky to survive.

On a Tuesday morning in February 2014, young neurosurgeon Dr Michael Wong had just entered the main foyer of the Western Hospital in the suburb of Footscray in Melbourne on his way to his regular out-patient clinic.[18] A man, later found to be one of his patients, attacked him from behind and stabbed him 14 times. Several staff members and a patient came to his rescue and were able to divert the attacker while Dr Wong was dragged by two people 150 metres to the safety of the Emergency Department. He spent ten hours in the operating theatre while severe injuries to his head, chest, abdomen, back, legs, arms and hands were attended to. The most life-threatening wound was to the chest where a major artery was bleeding. By chance, the hospital's visiting cardio-thoracic surgeon was in the hospital that morning and was able to attend the operating theatre immediately.

Dr Wong survived and, despite the injuries to his hands, he has been able to resume his career as a neurosurgeon. Three people who came to his aid, two staff members and a patient, were later awarded a Pride of Australia Outstanding Bravery medal. The assailant was a young man, a refugee, who suffered from paranoid schizophrenia. The man was not charged for the crime but was ordered to be kept in a high security psychiatric institute for a minimum of 25 years. Dr Wong has since been a strong advocate for improved security in our public hospitals as discussed in Chapter 14.

Three years later in May 2017 a surgeon at the Box Hill Hospital in suburban Melbourne was assaulted in the hospital entrance foyer.[19] Dr Patrick Pritzwald-Stegmann, a cardio-thoracic surgeon, had asked a group of young men to desist from smoking in a designated non-smoking area immediately outside the main hospital entrance. The men refused to move so Dr Pritzwald-Stegmann entered the foyer planning to seek the assistance of the hospital's security staff. One of the group followed him, there was a confrontation, and then without warning the man punched Pritzwald-Stegmann once to the head. The doctor, unconscious, fell without protection and struck his head on the tiled floor. He never regained consciousness and died four weeks later, leaving behind a wife and five-year-old twin daughters.

In 2018 in the Victorian Supreme Court, the 24-year-old man was found guilty of manslaughter and was sentenced to ten years and six months in gaol. He was the first person to be sentenced after the Victorian Parliament passed tougher laws for 'one punch' killings and as a result he will not be eligible for parole until 2028.

In June 2006 Dr Khulod Maarouf-Hassan was stabbed to death in her general practice in the Melbourne suburb of Noble Park. Dr Maarouf-Hassan, a qualified ophthalmologist in Syria, had emigrated to Australia in 1986 with her husband who was a veterinarian. She took on the difficult challenge of passing the Australian qualifying examinations and during these years she and her family ran a milk bar on the Mornington Peninsula. With the local examination out of the way, she successfully negotiated the path to independent medical practice, retrained as a general practitioner, and had recently become a Fellow of the Royal Australian College of General Practitioners. In her practice, she had established a fine reputation for her support for refugees and disadvantaged people.

Her attacker was a current patient, a young male refugee, who forced his way into her surgery and stabbed her 26 times. He was charged with her murder but after two hearings in the Supreme Court it was determined that because of mental ill-health (described as a delusional disorder) he was unfit to stand trial and instead was sentenced to 25 years in a high-security psychiatric institute.[20] This case also led to widespread demands to make medical practices safer.[21]

One of the most shocking murders of Australian doctors took place on Wickham Terrace in Brisbane in 1955. The murders were committed by an angry, revengeful, isolated and disturbed man, a 39-year-old German migrant named Karl Kast, who felt that he had been denied compensation for a back injury that had occurred at work. Wickham Terrace was a street where many of Brisbane's specialist doctors had their private consulting rooms, including several of the city's orthopaedic surgeons. Kast had consulted some of these surgeons so he knew his way around the area.

On the afternoon of 1 December 1955 he went on a rampage, armed with a .38 calibre pistol, 100 rounds of ammunition and 12 home-made pipe bombs. He found and shot three orthopaedic surgeons, two fatally. The survivor was a Dr Michael Gallagher and the deceased were Dr Andrew Murray and Dr Arthur Meehan. Kast sited three of his bombs at one office where a visiting patient, horse trainer George Boland, recognising what they were, threw them into the street but the last exploded in his hand leading to the loss of three fingers. Kast then moved to another building where he killed himself with his remaining bombs which caused a blast widely heard across the city.[22]

This book is primarily an account of the dangers faced by doctors and other health professionals. The murderous rampage summarised below is to remind readers that non-clinical staff can also be placed at risk from deranged and violent patients. On 12 November 1992, a psychotic man, William Jolly, who had formed the belief that a doctor's receptionist had taken a dislike to him, attended a private consulting complex at the Mercy Hospital in East Melbourne. He asked to see that receptionist. When informed that she was not there, he shot the receptionist who gave him the information four times in the head, killing her instantly.

He then went to another floor where he threatened another receptionist, Beryl Smith. She bravely sought to calm him but he shot her in the leg. Jolly then moved to other levels and all told fired 21 rounds of ammunition. When the police attended, he gave himself up. In court, he pleaded guilty to the charges but because of his mental ill-health was sentenced to 15 years detention in a psychiatric institute, with a minimum period of 10 years. Beryl Smith was later awarded the Australian Bravery Medal, Tattersall's award for achievement and the Royal Humane Society's

Clarke Gold Medal for her bravery in seeking to calm the deranged Jolly.[23]

For completeness, these are not the only settings in which doctors and their staff are at risk of violence while going about their duties. I am aware of the instance of a young Australian doctor, Dr Frank Shann, who was the sole paediatrician to one half of the population of Papua New Guinea. On a Sunday in 1981 he was pursuing a research project in the Goroka Base Hospital and came close to death from stabbing. A mentally disturbed man, armed with a knife in each hand, ran through the wards attacking patients and staff at random. Shann was stabbed eleven times, including a deep wound to the abdomen. He recalls trying to fend off the attacker with one hand while using the other to stop his intestines dragging on the floor. He slipped over in what he assumes was a pool of blood and intestinal content and so did the attacker. Their falls probably saved his life as he was then able to get away and find his way to the emergency department.

Three patients were killed by the attacker and several others were seriously wounded. Shann suffered enormous loss of blood. He had a cardiac arrest caused by blood loss, sedation and pancreatitis from a bisected pancreas. He was resuscitated and had life-saving surgery in Goroka. After a month, he was sufficiently well to be flown to the Royal Melbourne Hospital where he underwent further major surgery and was in hospital for another three months. Dr Shann made an amazing recovery, returned to Papua New Guinea to finish his research, and went on to a remarkable career in both research and clinical medicine, resulting in his receipt of an Order of Australia award.[24] His attacker, who suffered from schizophrenia, remained in a high security psychiatric hospital for the rest of his life.

There have been many other Australian doctors who were injured or killed while pursuing their profession. I refer to the large number of Australian doctors who volunteered to join the Armed Forces in the two World Wars. As non-combatants, they were theoretically protected from harm by the Geneva Convention and its predecessor but this did not prevent the sinking of an Australian hospital ship, the Centaur, off the coast of Queensland in 1943 with the loss of 268 lives, including eleven nurses and seventeen doctors.[25] Neither did the Convention prevent the execution of seven Australian doctors by Japanese soldiers.[26]

The tragic death of Sydney cardiac surgeon, Dr Victor Chang, in 1991 is a reminder that some doctors who become public figures are also at risk. Dr Chang had been identified very much at random as a possibly wealthy person who might be a suitable subject for an extortion attempt. His crude would-be extortionists, citizens of Malaysia, followed his car one morning, forced his car to pull over and demanded money. When a man in the street came forward to help Chang, one of the extortionists panicked and shot Chang twice in the head. Chang, the surgeon who undertook the first heart transplant operation in Australia, had been named as the Australian of the Century and thus this was a tragedy of the greatest proportions.[27]

Less well-known doctors than Dr Chang have also been the target of assault and robbery. Two junior doctors were assaulted in separate incidents in the same week at the Sunshine Hospital in Melbourne in 2019.[28] In both instances the doctors were walking to their cars that were parked near to the hospital. The motivation in each instance was theft and in one of the attacks, also the hijacking of the doctor's car. Any citizen could be similarly at risk but the proximity to a large hospital raises the possibility that they were targeted in anticipation that the individuals might be carrying valuable items such as drugs or money. These two attacks occurred despite the presence of security staff on the hospital grounds. Preventing similar assaults will require attention to the provision of adequate car parking for staff or the provision of security escorts to remotely parked cars.

Understandably after the above deaths of doctors at the hands of patients and random assaults on healthcare workers, there have been calls from the medical profession for steps to be taken to reduce the risks of such attacks in the future. Doctors who have survived attempts on their lives have been vocal in these matters. Suggestions have been made in regard to increased security presence in our hospitals, steeper penalties for offenders, education and advice for general practitioners about identifying and minimising risks, and enhanced identification of potential offenders. These and related possible preventive measures are discussed more fully in Chapter 14.

4

The risk of
blood-borne viruses

The term 'blood-borne' refers to the means by which a virus passes from one human host to the next, i.e. the blood or blood-contaminated fluid or other body fluid which contains the virus needs to penetrate through the strong barrier provided by human skin. Prior to the availability of accurate testing of donors, blood transfusion was the major known means of transmission of these viruses. Now in health care, transmission most often occurs via accidental penetration of the skin by a sharp blood-contaminated object, most often a venesection (blood-taking) needle. Such injuries are more likely to happen if the doctor is sleep-deprived[1] (see Chapter 12). Far less often, but still possible, is transmission via a splash of infected blood making contact with a mucous membrane such as that of the eye. Beyond the area of health care, spread of blood-borne viruses most often occurs in the sharing of needles and equipment among intravenous drug users. Spread is also possible via exposure of mucous membrane or abraded skin thus explaining transmission through unprotected sexual intercourse.

The best known and most commonly encountered blood-borne viruses are the human immunodeficiency virus (HIV) which causes the acquired immune deficiency syndrome (AIDS), and the hepatitis B and hepatitis C viruses. All three viruses have caused the deaths of doctors and other health-care workers via occupational exposure. As this chapter explains, the risk of death has been greatly reduced by a number of means over the last three decades. Nevertheless every health care worker, especially surgeons and those who make up the surgical team, must remain vigilant and maintain standard precautions (see below).

HIV/AIDS

Memories of dangerous happenings tend to fade over time. Younger readers will have no memories of the widespread fears in the 1980s of the universally fatal illness AIDS caused by the newly recognised human immunodeficiency virus (HIV) nor of the stigmatisation of persons infected with HIV. In the early phases, the HIV/AIDS pandemic brought out the best and the worst of most communities and the best and worst of the medical profession. HIV still infects many new individuals in Australia each year[2] and still poses risks of accidental spread to doctors, other health-care workers and laboratory technicians. However, fear of the virus has been greatly diminished predominantly because of the development of generally safe and effective antiviral medications. These medications, while not curing the infection, can ensure a normal lifespan. In the developed world, where antiviral medications are readily available and usually affordable, the ongoing existence of the risk of infection seems to be mostly ignored by the general population. Sadly in many developing countries where, without adequate public health measures and community education, and without sufficient access to affordable antiviral drugs, the pandemic continues with consequent high mortality rates and not just in homosexually active men.

For Australian doctors and the Australian community, the worst of the HIV/AIDS pandemic is well behind us. Nevertheless the story needs to be told and retold as there are many lessons that were learned that are likely be relevant to future viral pandemics. For doctors working in developing countries, there remain significant risks of contracting not only HIV but also infectious diseases such as tuberculosis and hepatitis C that can complicate AIDS. These risks extend to Australian medical students who undertake elective clinical placements in these countries.

The first awareness of this deadly new disease emerged in the USA in 1981. A number of young men became ill and died with a rare fungal lung infection, pneumocystis carinii pneumonia.[3] In the ensuing months, it became clear that these young men had two features in common; severely depressed immune systems and homosexuality. Within twelve months, in the USA nearly 600 cases were reported of whom almost half had died. Over that time it was also observed that the disease was not confined to sexually active homosexual men as it was found in intravenous drug users and in recipients of blood transfusions and blood products (the latter recipients included people with haemophilia). In 1982 the new disease was given the name of acquired immune deficiency syndrome (AIDS).

It was quickly recognised that the disease was transmissible and it was postulated that most probably it was due to a virus. This was confirmed almost simultaneously in research laboratories in France and the USA in 1983. The virus was given the name of human immunodeficiency virus (HIV). Gradually data was accumulated about the rate at which the disease progresses from the initial exposure to the virus through to death from AIDS. Data also accumulated about the infectivity of the virus. From the point in time of being infected, it can take three to twelve weeks for the virus to be detected in the blood via testing for HIV antibodies. Using testing for the RNA[4] of HIV, infection can now be detected much earlier.

Many newly infected people experience a seroconversion illness at two to four weeks which manifests as mild influenza-like or glandular fever-like symptoms and a rash. Otherwise, if not diagnosed, and not given antiviral medications, the infected person is likely to remain an asymptomatic carrier of the virus for several years before the immune system is attacked and weakened. Once this stage is reached, the HIV carrier is now at risk of a range of infections including pneumocystis, tuberculosis and hepatitis C as well as being at risk of a range of cancers, including the otherwise rare Kaposi sarcoma. In this symptomatic phase the person is deemed to be suffering from AIDS.

HIV is a blood-borne virus. Its most common mode of transmission in the developed world is via unprotected anal sex while in the developing world transmission is often via heterosexual intercourse. The virus can be transmitted in utero and thus some babies are born infected with HIV. It can also be transmitted via the sharing of needles by injecting drug users, by inadequate sterilisation of equipment in tattoo parlours, and by accidents with needles and other sharp instruments in hospitals and dental surgeries.

In the early years of the pandemic, blood transfusions also carried a serious risk, especially in those countries that paid their blood donors. There is also a very small risk if infected blood comes in contact with a mucous membrane, for example via the splatter of blood to the eye as can occur in the operating theatre.

For health-care workers, there was some reassuring news in the data that was soon accumulated about the infectivity of the virus. This came from studying thousands of nurses, doctors and others who had experienced a needle-stick injury where that needle had recently been used in a patient with proven HIV. Compared with hepatitis B (see below), HIV has a relatively low infectivity. Following a needle-stick injury only one person in 300 becomes infected while for exposure via the mucous membranes this falls to one in 1000.[5] The risk can be stratified if the viral load in the source blood is known.[6] Nevertheless, the weeks spent waiting to find out if one has been infected are made no less stressful by this statistical information. There are now strict protocols to be followed after needle-stick and other 'sharps' injuries. I will return to these after I have considered selected aspects of the early history of the AIDS pandemic in more detail.

In the 1980s this new illness provided several predicaments. The most worrisome was the universally lethal nature of the illness of AIDS and the absence of effective treatments; dealing with secondary infections such as pneumocystis and TB could only prolong life for months rather than years. Also distressing was the widespread stigmatisation of gay men and discrimination in their access to medical care. For doctors, other health-care workers, and laboratory scientists, there came the fear of the lethal infection being transmitted via contact with infected blood. Because the focus of this book is on the dangers that doctors may face in clinical practice, most of this chapter is devoted to this aspect but we should not forget the enormous loss of life, usually young life, occasioned by the HIV/AIDS pandemic[7] nor the harm that many fellow members of our community suffered through stigmatisation. Neither should citizens of developed countries forget that the HIV/AIDS pandemic is far from controlled in the rest of the world.[8]

Despite the fear engendered by untreatable and eventually fatal HIV infection and the deep concern that health-care workers might become infected and die of AIDS, the reality is that few health-care workers and very few doctors have died of AIDS contracted through their work. This is not to deny the tragedy of those deaths. Worldwide data on deaths from AIDS in health-care workers are not easy to find. The UK has reported four deaths of health-care workers from AIDS.[9] Data from the USA published in 2005 indicates that up to that year, 24 nurses and 12 doctors in the USA had died of AIDS contracted at work.[10] The report emphasised how incomplete was the occupational health data collected for healthcare workers but estimated that '*17–57 healthcare worker per million employed die annually from occupational infections and injuries*'. This mortality rate was well below that of construction workers (1,081–1,452) but above the rate for lawyers (7–14). The authors added '*Our results therefore may underestimate the actual occupational death rate for these diseases (in healthcare workers). Furthermore, these estimates do not account for deaths from other infections which demonstrate the problems engendered by the current lack of a national tracking system. This finding stands in contrast to the rigorous approach used to track occupational deaths of various other workers, such as police officers and firefighters.*'

Putting aside for the moment the terrible alarm and harm that HIV infection engendered for communities, there are aspects of the early days of the pandemic from which the health care system learned important lessons. Although not part of this book, there were also lessons that convinced many societies to enact measures to counter the gross discrimination experienced by subgroups of our communities who bore the brunt of the pandemic.

For the health care system and especially for the medical profession, the lessons lay in two distinct fields. The first was the focus that was brought to bear on the ethical dilemmas faced by a generally fearful medical profession. The second lay in prompting doctors and the systems in which they worked to do better in terms of 'infection control'.

In the USA where the pandemic first emerged, the widely debated ethical issue was whether doctors had an obligation to provide care for patients who were, or who might be, infected with HIV.[11] Those who argued that there was no such obligation used a range of premises, some of which now seem inventive. A major theme ran as follows. When they graduated, doctors in that era were aware that the care of patients could involve the doctor in exposure to an infectious disease. However this awareness was associated with an understanding that antibiotics, vaccinations and other measures had greatly reduced any serious risk to the life of the doctor. Thus it was argued that with the advent of a new lethal virus 'all bets were off'.

As an extension, it was also argued that the so-called social contract that doctors had with the community to treat all-comers was necessarily based on the informed consent of the doctor to accept the risks that were known at the time of joining the medical profession. As HIV/AIDS was new, and as the disease had not been part of the consent that they had given, doctors were now free to re-negotiate their social contract. Universally it seems to me that doctors who used this argument perceived a contract that was very one-sided. It is difficult to identify any occasion wherein the medical profession has actually involved the other side of this social contract, i.e. the community at large, in any negotiations or consultations. I know of a single exception in Australia and this occurred well after the AIDS pandemic.[12] Should the medical profession ever enter such negotiations, the profession may well find genuine understanding and willingness to compromise on the part of the broader community.

A second element of the case that some doctors put forward was to seek parallels with other situations where ethical codes absolved them of responsibility. Hence it was seriously argued that if a doctor in the USA was free to refuse to accept an uninsured patient then surely one could refuse to see a patient who carried HIV. Those who mounted such arguments seemed unconcerned that such refusal transferred the burdens and risks to the junior medical staff and those senior medical staff who had opted to work in the public hospitals of the USA.

There were other twists to these arguments. In drawing an analogy with fire-fighters and the military, it was held that even these professionals were not expected to be heroic. It was said that in dangerous situations, volunteers in these services were routinely called for. Thus by extension it was argued that HIV/AIDS patients should be cared for by doctors who volunteered to do so. I am sceptical of this analogy. In my view, the brave conduct of the New York fire-fighters in the 9/11 terrorist attacks in 2001 who did not hesitate to instantly respond to a dire emergency, despite the dangers, should permanently demolish the argument that only volunteers need be exposed to serious risk.

It was also argued that since doctors are an essential service, as many members as possible should be protected from risking their lives through being expected to care for HIV-infected patients. Analogies were even drawn with those cities during the plague era that sought to hire doctors for the express purpose of caring for victims of the plague.

These arguments found many supporters,[13] so much so that some US state medical boards advised that doctors could indeed choose to refuse to see HIV-infected patients and would suffer no consequences. Other medical boards took the opposite view as did several national medical organisations. These opposing viewpoints were based on a different interpretation of the implied social contracts that doctors have entered into and based on the long-standing ethical principle that doctors should always place the interests of the patient ahead of their own interest. Thus several major medical organisations including the American College of Physicians and the Infectious Disease Society of America were unequivocal about the physician's duty to treat.[14]

The debates on this subject were less emotive and less intense in Australia. I believe that there were a number of factors at work that engendered this difference. We had a stronger public hospital system with better access to care for every citizen, many of our major cities still had hospitals dedicated to the management of infectious disease, and there was a preparedness of sufficient GPs[15] and other specialists to take on this work. Striking in this milieu was the willingness of St Vincent's Public Hospital in Sydney to take a leading role both in the care of patients with AIDS and in supporting research in the disease, despite the Catholic Church's long-standing declaration that homosexuality activity was unacceptable.[16]

The HIV/AIDS pandemic provoked further improvement in approaches to minimising the risk of blood-borne infections in doctors, nurses and other hospital staff, paving the way for what were at first called 'universal precautions' and are now called 'standard precautions'. Doctors and nurses had for decades been aware of the need to use 'aseptic techniques' to stop patients being infected in the operating theatre, or during the changing of surgical dressings, or in performing investigative procedures such as a lumbar puncture. However, little or no attention had been paid to preventing transmission in the other direction, i.e. from patient to healthcare worker. Awareness of the possibility that hospital staff might accidentally infect themselves via contact with a patient's blood grew out of the discovery of the hepatitis B virus in 1966 and from that time on steps were gradually introduced to reduce the risk of transmission of the virus to others. The implementation of these steps was rapidly accelerated with the advent of HIV.

The ability to test for HIV and hepatitis B, and later hepatitis C, raised new ethical issues including the serious question as to whether any doctor who carried one of these viruses could safely be allowed to continue to practise and the parallel question as to whether patients had a right to be informed should their doctor harbour one of these viruses.

In the early phase of the HIV pandemic, some doctors, especially surgeons, at first argued that the safety of staff might be best ensured by insisting that patients be tested for HIV prior to any planned operation. Thus should a patient carry the virus, the surgical team could take additional care during surgery to avoid infecting themselves. This notion was short-lived on the grounds that it was discriminatory and stigmatising unless every patient was to be tested, and was impractical when surgery was required urgently. Consensus was soon reached that staff safety was best addressed by regarding every patient as possibly infectious and that all operating theatre staff would use 'universal precautions' at every operation. Now known as standard precautions, they especially involve the donning of personal protective equipment and strict adherence to the safe disposal of needles and other sharp instruments. These precautions are backed up by additional measures to be used to prevent transmission to staff of airborne or droplet infections in other infectious diseases.[17]

Of these measures, the most important change was also one of the simplest to institute; viz. the safe disposal of needles. A common situation for the risk of needle-stick injury was during the re-capping of used disposable needles. Re-capping was designed to prevent injury to other staff whose duty it was to collect and dispose of needles and other equipment. Re-capping was abandoned and instead wide-mouthed plastic receptacles were introduced for the disposal of all used 'sharps'. The receptacles were later incinerated. This single measure greatly reduced the incidence of injuries. Its introduction was not completely trouble-free as at first it was common practice for the receptacles to be placed at ground level; this was banned after reports appeared of young children putting their hands into the brightly coloured plastic bins.

Efforts have also been made to design safer equipment for venesection and related procedures (called safety-engineered devices). While this equipment has further reduced the incidence of needle-stick injuries, it must be supported by adequate training of staff. And there is some equipment such as the curved needles used in suturing that cannot be re-engineered for safety.

Needle-stick and other sharps injuries, while reduced in frequency, still occur and hospitals and other health-care workplaces have strict occupational health and safety protocols in place to deal with these incidents. The protocols depend entirely on the prompt reporting of any such injury; it seems that some doctors choose not to report and prefer to 'take their chances'.[18] The protocols are demanding as they involve urgent testing of the patient whose blood may be infective, base line testing for HIV, hepatitis B and hepatitis C in the now possibly infected health-care worker, and in high-risk situations, early – within hours – administration of antiviral drugs which are not free of side-effects.

The HIV/AIDS epidemic also influenced blood transfusion practices. Blood transfusion use was minimised or avoided where this could be done safely. Auto-transfusion was introduced whereby patients who were booked for surgery could donate their own blood to be stored for use when the time for the surgery arrived. Techniques for safely scavenging and re-infusing blood lost during an operation were also developed.

So far, I have addressed the risks of doctors and other health care workers contracting HIV from patients. However, from a community perspective, greater anxiety arose over the possibility that a doctor, especially a surgeon, who carried HIV might accidentally transfer the virus to the patient. There were some surgeons who contracted HIV, but unaware of their status, continued to operate. When the diagnosis became known, large numbers of their patients were recalled for testing for HIV, causing community alarm and political uproar, with some politicians insisting that all surgeons should be regularly tested.[19]

Addressing this anxiety led to two significant changes in practice. The first involved identifying surgical procedures where such risks were real (even if slight); these became known as 'exposure prone procedures (EPPs)'. EPPS are defined as *'procedures where there is a risk of injury to the health care worker resulting in exposure of the patient's open tissues to the blood of the HCW. These procedures include those where the HCW's hands (whether gloved or not) may be in contact with sharp instruments, needle tips or sharp tissues (spicules of bone or teeth) inside a patient's open body cavity, wound or confined anatomical space where the hands or fingertips may not be completely visible at all times'.*[20] EPPs carry two risks: the doctor may be infected by the patient's blood or the virus in the blood of an infected doctor may be transmitted to the patient.

The second change was agreement by surgeons undertaking EPPs to be regularly tested for the presence of HIV, hepatitis B and hepatitis C. In Australia initially, surgeons underwent these blood tests every six months, as well as after any sharps injury that occurred during surgery. National guidelines issued by the Communicable Diseases Network of Australia,[21] and backed by the authority of the Australian Health Practitioner Regulation Agency and the Medical Board of Australia, now call for testing at least every three years. Initially, surgeons found that the days waiting for their test results were extremely stressful, a reaction that was completely understandable. Until advances were made in treatments and in categorising the severity of any new infection, the surgeon knew that a positive result for any of these viruses would likely be the end of his or her surgical career and if the infection was HIV might also signal the end of his or her life. These were very difficult times for surgeons.

Surgeons in Australia who undertake EPPs are now subject to strict oversight by the Medical Board of Australia.[22] When renewing their medical registration each year, these surgeons are asked to declare that they are following the guidelines of the Communicable Diseases Network of Australia. Should a test for one of these viruses be positive, the guidelines state that the surgeon 'must cease performing EPPs immediately and seek appropriate medical care'. In most instances, thanks to advances in treatment and enhanced measurement of a doctor's viral load, the majority of surgeons are able to safely resume their careers. However, the stress and worry during the enforced time away from work until the situation is clarified must be a huge burden. While there are several well-documented instances of doctors who have accidentally infected patients with hepatitis B and hepatitis C (see below), instances of transmission of HIV to patients by surgeons are very rare.[23]

Lastly, the putative origin of HIV is of relevance since it provides a warning that humankind can expect to see new viral illnesses emerge unpredictably in the future. It is generally held that HIV crossed from non-human primates to humans in west central Africa possibly as early as the 1920s. Since the precise means of this viral 'escape' is unknown, we cannot plan measures to prevent future episodes of the escape of a virus from wild life that proves dangerous to humans. In searching back for evidence of the first documented death from HIV/AIDS, the farthest back reached so far is to 1959.[24] If the virus first crossed to man in the 1920s, as is held, it took sixty years for a new pandemic to unfold. This leads to the question as to what other potentially serious viral diseases are already in nature's pipeline?

The hepatitis viruses

There are several viruses that can cause hepatitis (inflammation of the liver). The best known and most frequently encountered are hepatitis A, hepatitis B and hepatitis C. Of these, the blood-borne hepatitis B and hepatitis C viruses are a risk for doctors and other health-care workers. Hepatitis A should not be a risk but is briefly described for completeness.

Hepatitis A, formerly known as infectious hepatitis, is not blood-borne but is spread by the faecal-oral route. Poor hand hygiene contributes to the spread of the virus. Community outbreaks have also followed contamination of oyster beds with sewage. While the virus may sometimes cause severe illness, death from hepatitis A is rare and with recovery comes lifelong immunity. The virus does not persist in the body and thus does not lead to cirrhosis or liver cancer, both of which are risks for hepatitis B and hepatitis C.

Hepatitis A in childhood is often asymptomatic or produces only minor non-specific symptoms so that the infection passes undiagnosed. The majority of Australians over 65 years of age are immune to the virus, based on childhood infection of which they were unaware. Spread among school children in more populated urban areas in the past was frequent. The fact that my childhood was spent in a remote rural part of Victoria may explain why my attack of hepatitis A came when I was an adult. It followed a brief holiday in Queensland in 1966 at the end of my first year after graduating as a doctor. Although I spent two weeks in hospital and was away from my duties as a second-year resident medical officer for two months, I was never severely ill and made a full recovery.

While it was long suspected that hepatitis A was caused by a virus, the virus was not identified until 1973.[25] The discovery soon led to the creation of an effective vaccine. The vaccine for hepatitis A is not part of the standard childhood immunisation program in Australia but is advised for selected groups of children and adults. These include Aboriginal and Torres Strait Islander children who live in areas where hepatitis A is endemic, non-immune Australians planning to travel to developing countries where hepatitis A remains endemic, and some people whose occupation or life-style place them at increased risk.

Hepatitis B and C are both blood-borne viruses and can be spread to healthcare workers by the same mechanisms already described above for HIV. For hepatitis B, there now exists an effective vaccine so infection of healthcare workers in Australia with the hepatitis B virus should be a thing of the past, assuming that mutant strains of the virus do not appear. Before entry to medical school in Australia, students are required to be vaccinated for hepatitis B or show evidence of immunity derived from past infection.[26] There is no vaccine for hepatitis C so doctors will remain at risk, especially those who undertake exposure-prone procedures.

I will describe first the intriguing history of the discovery of hepatitis B. This was formerly known as serum hepatitis, a name reflecting epidemiological evidence of a form of hepatitis with a long incubation period[27] linked to exposure to blood products. An important episode of illness that greatly improved our understanding of serum hepatitis was a large outbreak of hepatitis early in World War II that was traced to the use in troops of a yellow fever vaccine that had been stabilised with human serum. Because of good military record keeping, it was recognised that the incubation period for serum hepatitis was long, between 60 and 150 days. Later in that war, studies of outbreaks of infectious hepatitis (hepatitis A) in North Africa indicated that its incubation period was only 18 to 25 days. During the war and in the following two decades, further research studies, some later deemed unethical,[28] provided more information about serum hepatitis but the causative virus proved elusive.

A breakthrough in identifying a laboratory marker for the hepatitis B virus came serendipitously in 1966 when a US researcher, Dr Baruch Blumberg, then studying the genetics of blood groups, identified an unusual antigen in blood samples taken from Aboriginal Australians. Blumberg at first called this 'Australia antigen' but by 1969 it was recognised that rather than being a blood group antigen, it was a marker for serum hepatitis. Progress in research into hepatitis B after that point was rapid. By 1971 the virus itself had been isolated and analysed and by the mid-1980s, a safe and remarkably effective vaccine had been produced and approved for use.

Until a vaccine was developed for hepatitis B, the virus was a not infrequent cause of illness, some of it serious, among doctors and other health care workers, most often the result of needle-stick injury. In contradistinction to HIV, the hepatitis B virus is highly infectious. Exposure via a needle-stick penetration of the skin carries a risk of infection in the order of 6% to 30%. The risk varies with the number of viral particles in the patient's blood (viral load) and the subtype of hepatitis B carried. The illness contracted in this manner in adults is virtually always symptomatic and can be severe with symptoms including malaise, loss of appetite, vomiting, dark urine, jaundice and lethargy. Fatalities do occur although these are uncommon. Fortunately in adults infected via needle-stick injury, those who recover clear the virus and do not become long-term carriers, with rare exceptions. This is important for two reasons. First it obviates the risk of progression to cirrhosis or liver cancer. Second, once free of the virus, the doctor is no longer a risk to future patients.

Hepatitis B is still a common illness in many parts of the world. Being blood-borne, a frequent mode of transmission is from infected mother to baby during childbirth. Immediate vaccination of the newborn has greatly reduced the spread of the disease. In Australia it is routine obstetric practice to test every pregnant woman for hepatitis B.

Community transmission of hepatitis B is now rare in Australia. However there remain many adult carriers of the virus who are unaware of their status. These include people born overseas who were infected at birth and who have later migrated to Australia. Some will be identified should they seek to be trained as healthcare workers. Carriers of hepatitis B may transmit the infection via sharing of needles in drug use or by unprotected sexual intercourse. Vaccination has brought about the possibility of eventually eradicating hepatitis B, a goal now being actively pursued by the WHO.

While instances of a doctor infecting a patient with HIV are rare, there have been many reported cases where surgeons and dentists harbouring hepatitis B have transmitted the virus and deaths of patients have resulted.[29] These disturbing events (combined with the parallel concerns over the possible spread of HIV in those years) led to the introduction of universal precautions and regular testing of doctors and dentists undertaking exposure prone procedures. Surgeons found to be carriers were forced to abandon surgery. These days are now in the past through the uptake of vaccination, the development of effective anti-viral treatments, and the refinement of testing for the infectiousness of the blood of any doctor or patient carrying the virus. Australia has strict national guidelines,[30] supported and endorsed by the medical regulator, which apply to any health care worker who harbours hepatitis B. These permit surgeons to return to work when blood tests show undetectable viral loads. The guidelines make it clear that 'healthcare workers living with a blood borne virus may perform exposure prone procedures provided they comply with the guidelines.' This includes a requirement that each such healthcare worker remains under the close supervision of a medical specialist expert in managing blood-borne viruses.

Hepatitis C is the second blood-borne hepatitis virus that poses a risk to doctors and other healthcare workers. It was originally called non-A non-B hepatitis, the name given when the new laboratory test for hepatitis B helped researchers to recognise that a significant proportion of people who were ill with evidence of hepatitis contracted via a blood transfusion tested negative for hepatitis A and hepatitis B. It has taken some remarkable laboratory research to establish the identity of hepatitis C as a virus. The virus has not yet been cultured[31] and neither has a vaccine been created. On the positive side, great progress has been made in finding effective treatments.

As with hepatitis B, there have been instances of doctors infected with hepatitis C who have transmitted the infection to patients. The most notorious was a drug-addicted Melbourne doctor, James Peters, who infected 55 patients when aware that he carried hepatitis C. This came about because of his addiction to the anaesthetic drug, fentanyl. In preparing to give an anaesthetic, his practice was to draw up the drug into a syringe and inject himself before sharing the same needle, syringe and drug with the patient to be anaesthetised.[32] This distressing story has never been adequately investigated as Dr Peters pleaded guilty to criminal charges and a civil suit for damages was settled without any evidence being heard.

The presence and nature of the hepatitis C virus was determined in 1989 via a form of 'reverse engineering'. Using samples of liver taken from patients with non-A non-B hepatitis, researchers were able to reconstruct the genome of the virus (to extract all of genetic material of the virus). This allowed the development of accurate and sensitive tests for the virus. These tests were not only crucial for diagnosis but also for screening of blood donated for transfusion.

The illness caused by hepatitis C has many differences from hepatitis B. Only a small proportion of people infected with the virus experience the usual symptoms of hepatitis and even then, the symptoms may be minor. In addition, in contradistinction to hepatitis B, the body fails to clear the virus in 75–85% of people. The majority of these carriers of the virus remain free of ill-health for many years. During these years, if liver function tests are performed for any reason, the tests may show raised liver enzymes and this hopefully will prompt the doctor to test for hepatitis C. Routine screening for hepatitis C as occurs with blood donors and at risk populations such as intravenous drug users will identify carriers. For those people who are unaware of being infected, the diagnosis may not be made for decades when the development of cirrhosis of the liver, or concomitant cancer of the liver, finally leads to ill-health with attendant symptoms. In many countries, including Australia,[33] the end stage of hepatitis C (cirrhosis) is a common reason for liver transplantation.

Routine testing of blood donors has virtually eliminated the risk of contracting hepatitis C from a blood transfusion. In Australia, the major continuing source of transmission is through the sharing of needles by drug users. Other paths to infection that are seen uncommonly include via sexual intercourse, tattooing, mother to baby during birth or close contact after birth, and via sharing of contaminated items such as razor blades or toothbrushes. In developing countries, inadequate sterilisation of reusable medical equipment is a common source of infection.

The hepatitis C virus is less infectious than is hepatitis B as the risk of contracting the virus by healthcare workers after a needle-stick accident is estimated at around 2%. The risk is higher when the needle is hollow or where penetration of the skin has been deep.

The good news for patients and for infected healthcare workers is that there are now a range of effective antiviral medications (most taken orally for eight or twelve weeks) that can cure hepatitis C in up to 90% of cases. The drugs remain expensive and are therefore not likely to impact on the disease in developing countries where the prevalence of the disease can be as high as 3.5 % of the population.

In Australia, the prevention of hepatitis C in the healthcare setting relies on the measures used to reduce 'sharps' and needle-stick injuries described above. Reinforcement of the application of these measures remains vitally important. That 10% of people infected with the virus do not respond to antiviral drugs tells us why.

It is known that surgeons under-report needle-stick and other sharps penetration of their surgical gloves during surgery. This response is consistent with other forms of denial exhibited by doctors about their health. However for hepatitis C exposure, the earlier that infection is detected, the better the response to antiviral drugs.[34]

The information contained in this chapter shows that the dangers to doctors of becoming infected and of experiencing a severe or even fatal blood-borne illness have been significantly reduced in the last three to four decades. However, that risk is not zero and may never be. In addition, it should also be noted that doctors can suffer distress and psychological harm[35] from the necessary protocols to be followed after any exposure to a potential blood-borne virus, especially while awaiting the results of blood tests. I will return to the topic of stressors in medical practice in Chapter 8.

5

Viral respiratory illnesses

After the common cold, the next most frequently encountered respiratory infection is influenza. These are both viral infections for which antibiotics (antibacterial drugs) are ineffective. Although the 'great influenza' pandemic of 1918–1919[1] is well in the past, I begin this chapter by reminding readers how deadly that strain of the influenza (known now as Influenza A, strain H1N1) was in different successive waves and in different parts of the world during those two years. I do this because I have sensed a degree of denial of the severity of that pandemic, expressed by some commentators in terms of those events being in the pre-antibiotic era and before modern intensive care was developed and they have used these improvements to suggest that the deadliness of the great flu pandemic may never be repeated. I also sense some complacency related to the modern availability of vaccination against any current or predicted dominant strains of the influenza virus.

The great influenza pandemic eventually reached all parts of the globe. Entire settlements of Inuit people in the arctic zone died of the disease. It is held that a third of the world's population of 1.5 billion people were infected. The total number of deaths is not known but is estimated to be between 17 and 50 million or even higher. A large proportion of these people died a few weeks after the onset of their illness and their deaths were almost certainly due to secondary bacterial pneumonia, an infection that is now mostly treatable with antibiotics. However their numbers were such that even today our intensive care units, and hospitals more generally, would be overwhelmed.

More importantly, some commentators have ignored the significant numbers of otherwise healthy young people who died within 24 hours of becoming unwell, dying of what was most likely acute viral (i.e. influenzal) pneumonia accompanied by what is now called a cytokine storm.[2] These patients seemed to die of rapid onset respiratory failure, an illness now known as adult respiratory distress syndrome, accompanied by evidence of generalised bleeding.[3] Undoubtedly, some, but not all, of these young people may have been saved by access to a modern intensive care unit. Today, even with intensive care support, the adult respiratory distress syndrome has a mortality rate of around 40%.

Another forgotten aspect of the 1918–1919 pandemic was the impact on healthy young adults in whom the mortality rate was the highest. In the USA, 99% of deaths were in people under 65 years of age and almost 50% were in the age group of 20–40 years.[4] This was the reverse of previous outbreaks where the population most at risk was the frail elderly. This difference was attributed to immunity that had been acquired by older citizens from an influenza pandemic in 1889–1890.

This more rapid and distressing mode of death (influenzal pneumonia) was not seen in every country or in each outbreak in the 1918–1919 pandemic but was more likely to occur during any second wave of the illness. This is explained by the propensity of the influenza virus to mutate rapidly, with deadly strains appearing for brief periods. It is not an evolutionary advantage for the influenza virus to kill its host and thus mutations generally evolve such that less lethal strains are spread. While vaccination against the influenza virus gives protection against serious infection and transmission, there is no room for complacency as a new lethal strain may well appear again.

Australia fared comparatively well with the 1918–1919 pandemic, probably because of our remoteness and the timely use of quarantine. Even so, the death rate was reported as 2.7 per 1000 people. These must have included many Australian nurses and doctors. World-wide data on the mortality rate for doctors and nurses during the 1918–19 pandemic are not readily available. Given the above information about the mortality rate in people between 20 and 40 years of age, one must presume that some of the doctors and nurses also died young. There is no doubt that many nurses involved in the direct care of patients died.[5] It is also clear that nurses and doctors remained at their posts during the 1918–19 pandemic.

In 1918, viruses had not been discovered and the cause and mode of spread of influenza was unclear. We now know that the influenza virus is almost entirely spread from person to person through coughing or sneezing; the virus particles in tiny droplets can travel at least a metre through the air. Far less commonly, infection might result from contact with a surface contaminated with the virus (e.g. a tap handle, a door handle, or an eating utensil) followed by touching of the face.

The next major influenza pandemic occurred in 1957–58 and may have originated in China. It soon spread to nearby nations and was given the name of 'Asian flu'. The virus spread to most parts of the world and it was estimated that more people were infected than had been the case in 1918–1919. As a result between 1 and 4 million people died representing a mortality rate of less than 0.02%. By 1957, it was possible to manufacture vaccines effective against any new strain of the influenza virus. It is believed that the use of vaccination and the availability of antibiotics to treat the secondary bacterial pneumonia that could be lethal, especially in the elderly, were factors that reduced the impact of the Asian flu pandemic.[6]

There followed in 1968–69 the Hong Kong flu pandemic caused by a new variant, the H3N2 strain. The virus spread to most parts of the world and it was estimated that between one and four million people died. These numbers may seem high but it is claimed that the death rate was lower than for most of the earlier pandemics with a case fatality rate of 2 per 1000 people infected. The rapid production and distribution of a vaccine targeted at the new variant was an important control measure according to the World Health Organization.[7]

There was an influenza pandemic in 1977 which began in northern China but soon spread to Russia and beyond.[8] This was given the name of 'Russian flu' and was also the H1N1 strain, a strain that had not been seen for twenty years. School-children were the most susceptible group but fortunately the illness in children was mild.

The last influenza pandemic began in 2009 and was given the title of 'swine flu'.[9] Again this was due to the H1N1 strain but it was not a strain for which existing vaccines provided any protection. Although many people with underlying diseases died of the infection and the virus caused more severe illness in pregnant women, it was not seen as particularly lethal; the 1918–19 virus was thought to be 100 times more deadly. Rapidly developed targeted vaccines, new antiviral medications, and better understanding of the use of public health control measures probably contributed to this good outcome. There were no reports of deaths of doctors or other health care workers.

Beginning in the 1960s, the WHO has built a network of collaborating influenza centres enabling close monitoring of what has come to be called 'seasonal flu', looking for any shifts in the strains of the virus reported from around the world.[10] This sophisticated approach has allowed accurate predictions of future outbreaks with matching composition of the flu vaccines offered to at risk groups ahead of each flu season. Doctors and other health care workers are high on this list, both for their own protection and to minimise the risk of their spreading the virus to patients. However, uptake of the free vaccine by doctors is low,[11] perhaps reflecting their subconscious sense of invulnerability (see Chapter 7).

In addition the USA has supported important research into the 1918–1919 influenza virus. This project has enabled the 1918–19 virus to be re-constructed (in a specially designed containment facility at the National Institutes of Health). This research and other similar examples have been controversial because of the risk of laboratory escape and even bio-terrorism but may lead to greater understanding of influenza and further breakthroughs in vaccine development.[12]

There is little doubt that the world will see more pandemics of influenza. Australian Nobel Prize winner Dr Peter Doherty wrote in 2022 *'Given the size of the human population and the massive increase in passenger air travel, especially to and from countries that sell wildlife and live birds in open markets, there can be no doubt that we will suffer further pandemics'.*[13] Hopefully by virtue of access to timely new vaccines, doctors, nurses and other healthcare workers will be protected from whatever strain of influenza virus appears in the future.

But influenza is not the only potentially lethal respiratory viral infection that doctors will encounter. As mentioned in Chapter 1, in 2003 the world saw the first pandemic of a new illness of 'severe acute respiratory syndrome' (SARS). This was a frightening experience as the virus had not previously been known, was highly infectious, and caused many deaths, including among doctors and nurses. For those countries in which the virus predominantly spread (Hong Kong, China, Taiwan, Singapore, and Vietnam and Canada), it was a stark reminder of the risks that front-line workers may face. Sadly SARS was the cause of death of 46-year-old WHO expert on communicable diseases, Dr Carlo Urbani, who first identified SARS infection in an American businessman in Hanoi and who helped to promote greater global surveillance for this new virus.[14]

The illness originated in Guangdong province in China and was soon observed in Hong Kong. The symptoms were similar to those of influenza (i.e. fever, muscle pain, lethargy, cough and sore throat) but a larger proportion of sufferers progressed to experience shortness of breath from severe lung damage and needed respiratory support in intensive care. The mortality rate varied from country to country but was 11% in Canada, a rate much worse than for earlier influenza pandemics. Collaborative research in laboratories in Germany, USA and Hong Kong soon identified that the illness was due to a new virus that belonged to the Coronaviridae family (which includes the virus that causes the common cold).

The experience for Canada was restricted to the city of Toronto when two citizens flew home from Hong Kong with the virus, having stayed in a Hong Kong hotel alongside an infected doctor from Guangdong province. The outbreak was successfully contained to Toronto, but not before 438 people were infected and 44 died. Over 100 health care workers became ill, three of whom died (two nurses and a doctor). The alarming events and lessons learned by these Toronto hospitals and the healthcare system have been extensively described in the medical literature and were the subject of two government inquiries.[15]

I focus here just on some of those lessons learned and on the range of effects that the pandemic had on the staff of those hospitals. As described in

Chapter 1, for many nursing and medical staff the risk of returning home from work and infecting family members was so great that many chose not to go home between shifts. Most staff directly involved in the care of SARS patients found the experience stressful, not only because of their own risks and risks to their families but also through their knowledge that there was no treatment or vaccine and because it was unclear when or where the pandemic might end.

Initially there was no laboratory test and the diagnosis had to be made on clinical grounds. The incubation period for infection was only two to three days but as virtually every new case developed severe symptoms, contact tracing was straightforward. Problems were encountered over access to, and training in, the use of N95 respirator masks. There were also flow-on effects throughout the hospital system, clearly described in one of the two subsequent inquiries[16] as follows: *'Hospitals closed; cancer treatments and heart surgery were postponed. Patients were denied visitors. The sick and the dying suffered without the consolation of their families. The dead were disposed of quickly and in the absence of family and friends. The wider impact of SARS through cancelled heart surgery and delayed cancer treatments will never be known. And SARS was also an economic disaster for the country, the province and the Greater Toronto Area in particular.'*

Later in this report, Judge Campbell wrote: *'There was no system in place to prevent SARS or to stop it in its tracks. The only thing that saved us from a worse disaster was the courage and sacrifice and personal initiative of those who stepped up – the nurses, the doctors, the paramedics and all the others – sometimes at great personal risk, to get us through a crisis that never should have happened. Underlying all their work was the magnificent response of the public at large: patient, cooperative, supportive...'*

In the 2003 Toronto SARS 1 outbreak, two nurses and a doctor died. Across the world, 39 health-care workers died from SARS.[17] From combined data from four countries it was observed that over half the cases of SARS occurred in healthcare workers and medical students.[18] By 2017, Chinese scientists had traced the origin of the SARS 1 virus to cave-dwelling bats in Yunnan province. In their report they warned 'another deadly outbreak of

SARS could emerge at any time'.[19] The world was put on notice.

Judge Campbell completed his inquiry late in 2006. He understood that his report was intended to assist not only the Ontario hospital and healthcare system but also to warn other such systems throughout the world that they needed to be better prepared. His description of what happened in Toronto should surely have made this point clear: *'The Commission has not heard of any country or any health system that foresaw SARS. No one foresaw the sudden emergence of an invisible unknown disease with no diagnostic test, no diagnostic criteria, uncertain symptoms, an unknown clinical course, an unknown incubation period, an unknown duration of infectivity, an unknown virulence of infectivity, an unknown method of transmission, an unknown attack rate, an unknown death rate, an unknown infectious agent and origin, no known treatment and no known vaccine.*

SARS taught us that we must be ready for the unseen. That is one of the most important lessons of SARS. Although no one did foresee and perhaps no one could foresee the unique convergence of factors that made SARS a perfect storm, we know now that new microbial threats like SARS have happened and can happen again.'

The Toronto experience was in effect a trial run for the 2020 Covid-19 pandemic to which I now turn and through which we are still living. How many of the lessons from Toronto were taken to heart by Australian health authorities will only become clear when the inevitable national inquiry is conducted.

However before discussing the impact of the Covid-19 pandemic on Australia I need to insert the finding in 2012 of yet another respiratory virus which has been called the Middle East respiratory syndrome (MERS), first detected in Egypt. It too is a corona virus for which the reservoir is likely to be the camel. Fortunately it is not highly infectious and spread depends on close contact. On the other hand the virus is deadly as over a third of cases have died.[20] Limited spread to other countries such as South Korea via returning travellers has been reported. No cases have been detected in Australia but this may change when high volume travel to Mecca for the annual Hajj recommences.

Returning to the theme of Covid-19 I will only seek to describe the impact of the pandemic on health-care workers (doctors in particular) and will not dwell on the myriad of other issues that arose over the last three years. Some of those elements were remarkable, most noticeably the rapidity with which a number of effective and safe vaccines were developed. Some elements were distressing such as the fatal spread of the virus through aged care facilities in Australia. And some were disappointing when political 'games' were played by several senior politicians, egged on by some elements of our media.

It is still early days in the study and analysis of the impact of Covid-19 on Australian doctors. In some respects, our doctors have been saved the sort of outcomes seen in other developed countries.[21] To date, to my knowledge no practising Australian doctor has died of Covid and only a small number became quite unwell. This contrasts with the sad data from Italy where over 150 doctors died, with the UK where over 50 doctors died and with India where nearly 800 doctors died. With regard to Italy, the burden rapidly fell on older GPs working in smaller hospitals when the major hospitals were over-run. Not only was age a risk factor, but lack of personal protective equipment (PPE) and unfamiliarity with its use also probably contributed. Still not known is whether in the Italian phase of the pandemic the Covid strain was more lethal than the strains that later reached Australia.

It seems that those few doctors in Australia who did become infected with Covid probably caught the infection away from the hospital environment.[22] The availability of PPE and its proper use and subsequently the availability of vaccines presumably contributed to this good outcome.

Undoubtedly the pandemic greatly stressed health care workers in Australia, especially those at the front line: in general practice, emergency departments, intensive care units and public hospitals generally. In the surveys published so far, several aspects are noteworthy. Junior doctors reported higher levels of stress, anxiety and depression than did their seniors and for junior doctors these levels were higher than those reported in pre-pandemic surveys.[23] Most junior doctors did not seek formal help for mental ill-health issues for the predictable reasons of not having the time, not wanting to let their colleagues down and for fear over career progression (see Chapter 8). Because of the pressures of workloads, junior doctors experienced a lack of access to their usual peer and family support, as well as lack of opportunities to undertake stress-relieving activities through sport or other activities. An unexpected additional pressure on junior doctors was that many felt shunned by non-medical friends because the doctors were seen as potential spreaders of Covid virus.

The concerns of the junior doctors were much more centred on the risks to their families than to themselves. While this altruism is admirable, it may reflect to a considerable extent the armour of invulnerability that medical students and junior doctors unconsciously adopt (see Chapter 7). The altruism of junior doctors also extended to dangerous levels of presenteeism,[24] which answers the question that I posed myself at the outbreak of the pandemic. These young Australian doctors did not shirk their ethical obligations.

The pandemic has severely limited the learning opportunities for medical students and disrupted their examinations. Similarly, for junior doctors who had reached the stage of studying for and sitting their postgraduate examinations, their career paths have been similarly disrupted. The long-term consequences of these disruptions for medical students and trainee doctors remain to be seen.

6

Less common dangerous infectious diseases

Much of this chapter relates to recently emerged dangerous infectious diseases that so far have not breached Australia's defences. Most of these diseases are viral and not bacterial.[1] The defences that Australia relies on include being a large and remote island continent, having tight controls on the importation of live animals and certain foodstuffs, and the prompt introduction of quarantine in the face of new pandemics. Many of the diseases discussed below have caused the deaths of doctors and health care workers in other countries and therefore deserve attention. Australia's doctors may not be forever safe from these diseases. In addition, the many Australian doctors and medical students who seek to broaden their experience overseas or participate in health projects to assist developing nations need to be aware of these risks as do other Australians who plan to visit these countries.[2]

Most of these infectious diseases have only been recognised in recent decades. In nearly every one of these new viral infections in humans, research has shown that each virus lives normally in an animal species and at some point has crossed to infect humans. Epidemiologists speak of an 'animal reservoir' for each virus. Thus the reservoir for the influenza A virus is waterbirds, for SARS1 corona virus it is bats, for HIV it is non-human primates, and for Hendra virus it is probably bats and horses. As there are many animal viruses yet to be discovered and as humans further encroach on animal habitats, it has to be assumed that we will see new virus infections that cross from animals to humans. Some of these may also prove to be lethal.

The most extensively studied of this group of viral infections are the haemorrhagic fevers, of which the best known is Ebola virus. The natural reservoir for Ebola virus is believed to be the fruit bat. The illness was first reported in humans in the sub-Saharan African nations of South Sudan and the Democratic Republic of the Congo in 1976 and there have since been outbreaks in several neighbouring countries. As the name 'haemorrhagic fever' implies, this illness involves the onset of high fever and later extensive bleeding. The bleeding can take the form initially of tiny bleeding spots in the skin all over the body followed by overt bleeding from the lungs, the intestinal tract and elsewhere. Diarrhoea and dehydration contribute to the deaths of patients. Until recently there was no specific treatment but the outcomes were better if intravenous rehydration was available. Even then, the infection progressed rapidly to death in two-thirds of those infected. Two antiviral drugs have been approved for treatment in the USA but because of their cost, few patients in African countries are likely to receive these. A vaccine has also been developed and has begun to be deployed in at risk countries.

Ebola is not a respiratory virus spread by coughing but is thought to enter the body via breaks in the skin or via the mucous membranes of the mouth, nose and eyes. This can happen from direct physical contact with a patient, a deceased patient[3] or when a person comes into contact with the blood or secretions of a patient. This can happen in caring for a patient or in handling a corpse or a laboratory specimen. It is estimated that to 2020, around 33,604 Ebola virus infections had occurred in humans, including 14,742 deaths (average case fatality rate 43.8%), although case numbers differ slightly from source to source.[4] Ten percent of these deaths were in healthcare workers.[5]

In 2014 following outbreaks in Guinea, Liberia, and Sierra Leone, the Lancet reported 17,000 deaths of whom at least 600 were healthcare workers. The Lancet article provided summaries of the lives of twelve senior doctors, leaders of their profession, who died from Ebola. The article deserves to be widely read as it dramatically emphasises the dangerous lives that some doctors have to live.[6]

To date, there have been only three reports of Ebola being diagnosed outside Africa (two in the USA and one in Scotland), all involving persons who had recently travelled in Africa. As the incubation period after contact with the virus can extend to up to three weeks, and as the early symptoms are non-specific (usually fever, sore throat, muscle pain, and headache), a history of recent travel must be sought in any patient who presents with a febrile illness.

One of the patients in the USA transmitted the Ebola infection to two nurses, both of whom survived. It is only a matter of time before Australia sees a case. Anti-viral treatment is not yet widely available so protection of nurses and doctors caring for any patient is essential. This involves the use of personal protective equipment that covers all exposed skin and mucous membranes. Fortunately the same equipment has been crucial in protecting hospital staff from Covid-19 (which is much more readily transmitted than Ebola) so theoretically Australia should never see local transmission of the Ebola virus.

The family of viral haemorrhagic fevers is large and illnesses in humans due to the various viruses have been observed not only in Africa but also in Mexico, several South American countries and in Europe. Dengue fever belongs to this family as does yellow fever (see Chapter 2). Dengue fever, a mosquito borne disease, is endemic in Pacific Island countries and has been reported in Queensland. With climate change, dengue fever may spread further south in Australia.[7] Other haemorrhagic fevers include Lassa fever, Marburg virus and West Nile Fever (the last, also mosquito borne).

Of these the most deadly is Marburg virus. The virus was first discovered after an outbreak of a severe illness among laboratory workers in the German town of Marburg in 1967.[8] Several workers died. The infection was traced to African monkeys that had been imported from Uganda for research purposes. More recent research has traced the natural reservoir of the Marburg virus to the African fruit bat. Outbreaks have since been reported in a number of African countries. The course of the illness and the mode of human-to-human transmission have much in common with Ebola Virus disease, with a high mortality rate and deaths among health care workers.

The last viral infection to mention is Hendra virus which is one of the more recent discoveries of yet another fatal virus that has crossed to humans from an animal reservoir. It is also of interest because it was discovered in the Brisbane suburb of Hendra in 1994. The virus causes illness predominantly in horses. The natural reservoir for the virus is the Australian fruit bat, also known as the flying fox. Those who work closely with horses are at risk as the virus can be transmitted to humans. To date only seven people in Queensland have been infected but in four cases the illness was fatal.[9] The initial symptoms of Hendra virus infection mimic those of influenza with later progression to high fever, headache, and drowsiness, indicative of the development of meningitis or encephalitis with death to follow.[10] So far human to human transmission has not been reported. Since the precise path of infection from an infected horse to humans is not known, doctors and nurses caring for any patient with suspected Hendra virus infection need to use personal protective equipment.

Finally, I need to mention an old bacterial disease of which young Australians probably have little awareness, viz. tuberculosis. It is included in this chapter because in Australia it is now a 'less common infectious disease' as it is well-controlled here and is usually readily treated. It is only eighty years since it was untreatable and often lethal. My maternal grandmother died of TB in Melbourne when my mother was eleven years of age. Up until the discovery of the new antibiotic streptomycin in the 1940s, many Australian medical students and doctors spent months in special isolation hospitals established for TB patients and some died of the disease.

Tuberculosis is caused by mycobacterium tuberculosis. It is spread by small particle aerosols expelled from the lungs through coughing, sneezing or spitting. For pathologist-doctors and other mortuary room workers it can also be spread if due care is not taken when performing an autopsy on a person who has died of TB. The disease primarily affects the lungs but can spread to other sites including bone, brain and kidneys. In a high proportion of infected persons, the infection remains latent, meaning that the person has no symptoms and unless tested with a skin test[11] will remain unaware of their infection. If the infection becomes active (most likely to happen in immune-suppressed individuals, whether immune-suppressed from AIDS or via poverty and malnutrition) the usual symptoms include cough, sputum production which may be blood-stained, weight loss, night sweats and tiredness.

It is estimated that 25% of the world's population have TB, nearly all in the latent form. It remains a major public health problem in Africa, Southeast Asia and the Western Pacific. This needs to be kept in mind when medical students or doctors move from any of these regions to study or work in Australia. Should latent TB reactivate, the disease could be spread to patients.[12] TB reactivation is common in patients with HIV infection. In parts of Africa active TB remains prevalent and strains that are resistant to all drugs have emerged. As a result healthcare workers in some African countries are again dying of TB.

TB has not disappeared in Australia and is still an occupational hazard for doctors. Multi-drug resistant TB is increasingly common in our near neighbours, especially PNG, and healthcare workers, including students on electives, are at risk of contracting a potentially incurable infection.

In preparing this book I became aware for the first time that three Australian medical colleagues have been treated for TB or latent TB in the past. All had contracted the infection through clinical work. One was unwell with a pleural effusion and required hospitalisation and an invasive procedure to make the diagnosis. Fortunately in all three cases the strain of TB was not multi-drug resistant, antibiotic treatment was effective and only one suffered a side-effect of the therapy. Two did not need to isolate and lost no time from work. Two needed six months of quadruple anti-tuberculous medication. The third doctor, with latent TB, was prescribed the drug isoniazid for 12 months but the treatment was ceased prematurely when liver function tests became abnormal. The tests promptly returned to normal but when the doctor later sought to purchase disability insurance, this was refused – an unforeseen negative outcome of a work-related health issue. Finally it needs to be emphasised that if resistant strains of TB become common in Australia, these good outcomes for infected doctors will no longer be assured.

The physical health of doctors: Some good news

I have chosen to write separate chapters about the physical health of doctors as distinct from their mental health. I have done this for two reasons. First, some of the news about physical health of doctors is positive, while the news about mental well-being is decidedly negative. What may surprise many readers is that even for physical illnesses which generally carry little or no stigma, access to good medical care can be problematic for doctors. I felt that this second aspect, viz. barriers to good care, needed to be explored and understood before I sought to address mental ill-health issues where the role of barriers and stigma is greater and more complex.

Several studies show that doctors live longer when compared with similar professional groups. They are less likely to die of lung or liver disease but more likely to die of vascular disease or suicide. Another study shows that the health overall of female doctors is better than that of females in other professional groups.[1] Possibly this is because female doctors are more proactive in practising what they preach in regard to preventive medicine. Otherwise, to what extent this increased longevity, especially in male doctors, reflects their theoretical ready access to good medical care and/ or their capacity for early self-diagnosis is debatable. Opinion favours the likelihood that the longevity of doctors is mostly related to the health benefits that come with social class and higher incomes.

Here are some of the reasons for that opinion. Doctors generally and male doctors in particular often do not have a recognised GP,[2] do not participate in regular health screening, and many do not avail themselves of standard vaccinations recommended for healthcare workers.[3] Many doctors refer themselves to specialists (permissible under Medicare regulations) and many prescribe for themselves (illegal in Victoria and the Northern Territory). The vast majority of doctors have self-prescribed[4] at some point in their careers.

Many doctors, junior and senior, especially if hospital-based, also are inclined to use what are known as 'corridor consultations'; i.e. the seeking out of a colleague at work for advice about a personal health matter. While such action is tempting and even understandable for a busy doctor, it never represents good medical practice as any assessment by way of history taking or physical examination is necessarily superficial, no records are kept, and there is usually no follow-up.

One area of preventive medicine in which doctors performed well, especially in Australia, was to lead the way in giving up smoking tobacco once data became available in regard to lung cancer and heart disease. As a medical student in the early 1960s, I attended ward rounds where the senior physician or surgeon conducting the round would smoke in the hospital wards and nobody blinked an eyelid!

While almost no Australian doctors smoke tobacco these days, less progress has been made in regard to alcohol use and misuse. Research consistently reveals a prevalence of alcohol abuse of 10–17% in doctors. Also by virtue of ease of access, doctors are at increased risk of misuse of, and addiction to, narcotic pain killers and related drugs. These issues are discussed in more detail in Chapter 9.

I readily admit that I did not have my own GP until I was around fifty years of age. At that time, I thought that I needed reading glasses so I simply referred myself to an eye specialist. She found a small retinal haemorrhage which was most likely due to unrecognised high blood pressure. She asked when I last had my blood pressure checked. My answer of 'ten years ago' probably did not surprise her. I was a doctor after all.

I then referred myself to specialist physician who confirmed the diagnosis and prescribed an antihypertensive medication. He wisely advised me that I needed to find a GP as it was not his role to regularly review this medical issue. It proved to be a turning point in my attitude to the health problems of doctors and I remain grateful to him for his advice. I became a strong advocate for every doctor to have their own GP. A late convert, but better late than never!

In the thirty odd years since that experience there have been many more calls for every doctor to have a GP. Medical student education now covers the importance of looking after one's own health. However there has been little progress in the proportion of doctors who have their own GP with the figure hovering at around 50%.[5] Female doctors are more likely to have a regular GP, possibly because of their need for medical care relating to family planning and childbearing.

Another issue worthy of attention is the reality of self-diagnosis, self-prescribing and self-treatment by doctors. Many studies have confirmed this reality. I too have been guilty of this practice. We should not be shocked by such findings as this is what every citizen does, until they decide that they need to see a doctor. The major difference between those citizens and doctors is that the former can only purchase over-the-counter (OTC) medications from their pharmacist while the latter can readily access prescription-only drugs. I have some sympathy for doctors who self-treat, especially for presumed minor illness. They are not cluttering up general practice, they are remaining at work, and they are saving Medicare money. Problems arise when doctors self-prescribe prescription-only drugs and especially when those drugs include antidepressants, sedatives and narcotics. In these situations there is a hazardous absence of objective independent medical input into any diagnosis.

Why do most doctors subconsciously, and at times even consciously, see themselves as invulnerable to sickness and perhaps even immortal? Surely given their medical education, they of all people should be aware of the importance of preventive medicine, health screening, early diagnosis, and having their own GP? Whatever factors are at work, their impact must be considerable as these attitudes and the consequent behaviour are totally contrary to the expectations of the *Code of Conduct* of the Medical Board of Australia. In section 11 of the *Code*, doctors are told 'it is important for you to maintain your own health and wellbeing. This includes seeking an appropriate work-life balance'. This is followed by advice about having one's own GP, not self-prescribing and another six related invocations.[6]

This question as to how these attitudes arise has long intrigued psychologists who work with distressed doctors and who undertake research into doctors' health. Here is a brief summary of what psychologists believe happens to most young people when they set out to join the medical profession.

For many medical students, the reality of death and their own eventual mortality may first hit home when early in their medical course they are expected to dissect a human cadaver. From this point onwards, for students to be able cope with such a novel and strange experience, many sense a need to ignore or suppress any emotions, apprehensions or other feelings.[7] Such a response is reinforced by the desire to conform to the responses of their peers. Who will have the courage to be different? In this manner, via denial and suppression of any emotions, these future doctors are already subconsciously separating themselves from the rest of society and looking forward to becoming part of a profession that society generally admires and respects.

Even in those medical schools that have abandoned the dissection of cadavers to teach anatomy, there will be many occasions in the early years of the medical course where suppression of emotions by students must be the norm. These medical students understand, subconsciously if not consciously, that in speaking with and examining people who are likely to die, including sometimes ill people of their own age, they must suppress any feelings of anxiety or distress if they are ever to join the medical profession. The unacknowledged effects of interviewing and examining patients who are likely to die may be even greater if a family member of the student, now or in the past, is suffering or has suffered from the same or a similar fatal illness. The impacts of these experiences are not universally identical among medical students. Research has shown that the individual responses are influenced by childhood experiences and by the psychological make-up of the student (e.g. extrovert vs. introvert and other traits).

One of the first to study the psychologic vulnerabilities of doctors was US psychiatrist, Dr George Valliant, whose research group from the 1960s onwards closely followed a cohort of new medical graduates along with a comparison cohort of graduates in other fields.[8] His team was able to show that childhood experiences played a large role in the reasons for many students choosing a medical career and that these experiences also had an impact on such matters as the capacity of the doctor to be caring and empathic, and their vulnerability to many of the adverse consequences of the stress of medical practice. His findings are especially relevant to the next chapter on the mental well-being of doctors.

This subconscious need to be a doctor who is invulnerable, and the associated need to deny possible ill-health, pervades many aspects of doctors' lives. Doctors also find the role of being a patient difficult, for one cannot be both a doctor and a patient at the same time.[9] Equally many doctors find the role of being a treating doctor for other doctors difficult. Problems can also arise for the children of doctors, especially if both parents are doctors. Delays in diagnosis are common experiences in these families, whose children may never have attended an independent GP.

Both as medical students and later in their careers doctors will become aware that some illnesses are stigmatised by colleagues. Worse, they may find that even colleagues who have experienced the same or similar health problems are unsupportive, probably because of the pervasive influence of denial.[10]

In addition to the innate factors of invulnerability and denial that may delay access to care, doctors face additional barriers to obtaining good medical care. A Canadian report listed twelve identifiable barriers[11] and an Australian systematic review of the world literature published in 2008 provided a similar list of barriers.[12] Some of these obstacles exist for all patients and include embarrassment, fear of serious illness and fear of loss of income. For doctors there are additional concerns over privacy and confidentiality (for example, being seen by one's patients in the waiting rooms of another doctor), feelings of guilt for being away from duty, awareness that some illnesses carry stigma in the eyes of other doctors, and apprehension that under mandatory reporting laws (see Chapter 11) their health issue may be reported to the medical regulator.

These obstacles may be heightened for doctors in training and for medical students. Doctors in training are expected to work long hours and be available to patients, nursing staff and their senior consultants during these hours. Thus making time for appointments to see a GP or a specialist can be very difficult without drawing attention to their health issues. In addition, to be perceived as being unwell and even unreliable because of ill-health may undermine progression in their training. Similar fears exist for medical students who are reluctant to draw attention to their health problems.

For multiple reasons, trainee doctors are also reluctant to stay at home when unwell. They do not wish to let their colleagues down and they are very aware that hospital human resources departments have little or no capacity to replace junior medical staff at short notice.[13] Thus this informal training for 'presenteeism'[14] starts early. There is solid data to show that throughout their careers doctors take fewer sick leave days than do other professionals.[15]

This professional behaviour, while admirable in some ways, is not in anyone's best interests as working while unwell has been linked to an increase in needle-stick accidents and prescribing errors. And, if the illness is an infectious one, these doctors may be placing patients at risk.

To date there has been little done in Australia to examine and seek to reduce these obstacles to good quality care. Some workshops have been offered to help support doctors in the task of being a treating doctor for other doctors and some useful guidance on this role has been published by Dr Narelle Shadbolt and Dr Hilton Koppe. In addition, the AMA's Doctors for Doctors website offers an on-line training module which seeks to give similar guidance.[16] There are few lessons to be learned from other countries although the existence in Barcelona in Spain of a hospital solely for doctors and nurses caught my eye as did a formal training program in Norway for selected GPs to become more skilled in caring for doctors.[17]

These are just the obstacles that doctors face in regard to their physical health. In the next chapter I will address the even greater obstacles that doctors encounter when needing assistance with mental health issues.

The mental health of doctors: Not a happy picture

The information available about the mental health of medical students and doctors (junior doctors in particular) is disturbing. Mental health problems may be present before commencing medical school or begin during medical school[1] and increase during the early years after graduation. The assessment of prevalence depends primarily on self-reported responses to surveys but the reality of those responses is backed up by the objective experiences of the attendance of medical students and junior doctors at doctors' health programs.[2]

Burn-out (defined below) has been reported in up to 50% of Australian medical students, depression in 18% and suicidal ideation in 10%. A 2009 survey[3] of Australian junior doctors reported low job satisfaction in 71%, burn-out in 69% and compassion fatigue in 54%. The 2013 Beyond Blue survey[4] of the mental well-being of doctors of all categories reported depression in 21% of doctors. Other studies have reported a prevalence of depression in up to 60% in practising doctors and reported that 4% of medical students and 2% of doctors had made a suicide attempt at some point in their lifetime.[5] The Beyond Blue survey's opening statement reads: *'Doctors reported substantially higher rates of psychological distress and suicidal thoughts compared to both the Australian population and other Australian professionals'.*

The mental health problems of medical students and junior doctors are universal as comparable data can be found pretty much wherever one likes to look. Much data has come from the UK, USA, Canada and Norway that closely resembles the Australian data.[6] A meta-analysis[7] of data collected from several countries reported the average prevalence of suicidal ideation among medical students as 11%.[8] From Canada came a report about junior doctors in a family medicine (GP) training program of whom 33% admitted to experiencing suicidal ideation, 18% disclosed having a plan on how to take their own life, and 3% had attempted suicide.[9] In the last two years, the SARS Covid-19 pandemic has exacerbated the stresses experienced by doctors and other healthcare workers, especially for junior doctors and medical students (see also Chapter 5).

To me this looks a lot like a pandemic of mental ill-health. I wonder if anything comparable is happening to trainees in other health care professions or among police cadets and the like? We are all aware of alarm about the suicides of armed services veterans, and the subsequent Royal Commission. Perhaps we need a Royal Commission or in-depth inquiry into medical student and junior doctor mental health? I will return to this possibility in Chapter 14.

There have been responses in Australia and overseas to this unhappy picture but, in my view, to date the responses have focussed on seeking to better prepare junior doctors for the stresses ahead or on improved support for distressed medical students and junior doctors[10] and not on the conditions under which they study and work. To my mind a particularly relevant example of this inappropriate response is a lauded[11] USA internet-based approach offering cognitive behavioural training to interns to reduce suicidal ideation.[12] This is a prime example of the lack of attention given to the study and work environments which generate much of the distress that junior doctors experience.

As I have detailed in the previous chapter, from early in their careers medical students and doctors unconsciously or consciously develop an emotional armour to allow them to deal with events that might otherwise overwhelm them and impede their capacity to efficiently care for their patients. Overall this is a necessary development but it has its downsides. It contributes to doctors' denial of their own illnesses and to delays in diagnosis and treatment when they themselves become unwell. For some it is accompanied by a gradual decline in empathy. Meanwhile those doctors who maintain their empathy and conscientious attitude to caring are at greater risk of the mental health issues that I am about to describe. A certain amount of denial or temporary suppression of emotions and anxiety can be healthy and protective, but when denial is unconscious and over-relied upon as a defence mechanism it is inevitably harmful.

These unconscious influences may lead doctors to see themselves as different from their patients and thus invulnerable to illness, be it physical or mental. This tendency to denial becomes even more problematic when issues of possible mental ill-health arise. Now stigmatisation, embarrassment, feelings of failure, lack of support from colleagues who are equally in denial, fear regarding progression in career, and fear of the medical regulator play an even larger role in creating barriers to seeking help.

The conscious and subconscious reasons for young people wanting to become doctors and the selection criteria for medical students only add to the risk of mental ill-health. One UK study of reasons for selecting a medical career reported among four main reasons 'a need to be indispensable'.[13] As described recently by Gerada, medical students are selected in part for their 'perfectionistic, obsessional, compassionate traits'.[14] While these traits may make them altruistic and dedicated doctors, they also can predispose these people to continue to work while unwell, further delaying help, and sometimes placing their patients at risk. These same traits are linked to self-criticism and risk of depression.

Overseas-trained doctors (OTDs) who come here as migrants, or refugees, or to fill 'positions of need' (usually in rural or remote Australia) are even more likely to experience these stresses and mental health issues, particularly if English is not their first language or if they have trained and worked in countries with very different cultures, including the culture of medicine.[15] Added to the stress of settling in a new country are the difficulties in passing the examinations for medical registration in Australia and the discrimination many OTDs face from prejudiced Australians, even to the extent of being more likely to be the subject of complaint to the medical regulator. It is not difficult to imagine OTDs fearing to seek medical help for mental distress or illness in the presence of Australia's mandatory reporting legislation (see Chapter 11).

Some of the mental illnesses that I describe below can be accompanied by varying degrees of impairment and consequent inability to safely practise medicine. Delay in seeking help for mental ill-health not only harms the doctor but may also lead to harm to their patients. For this reason, medical boards and medical regulators have a vital role in protecting patients from such harm. For medical boards around the world, it has long been recognised that finding the right balance between the interests of protecting the public versus supporting distressed and unwell doctors to ensure their early access to help and return to work is never easy.[16] In Australia since 2010, I sense that the balance has been tilted too far one way. This important matter is addressed in Chapter 11.

As I will discuss later in this book, seeking to minimise stigmatisation of mental illness should be the goal of all involved in the health care system and especially in the agencies that are charged with regulating the medical profession. No doctor ever deliberately sets out to become mentally unwell. These mental health issues for doctors are all about being human and should never be regarded as signs of weakness. As Drs Epstein and Privitera wrote in 2019: '*Clinical work is stressful and always will be. Physicians are remarkably resilient, having survived the long path through medical training. They function well under duress – up to a point.*'[17]

Awareness of the mental health issues of medical students and doctors has grown considerably in the last 20 to 30 years. However, with rare exceptions, the responses to the issues have been ineffective. In reality, for junior doctors, the only thing that has changed has been a reduction in rostered working hours.[18] This well-motivated change had had at least two unintended negative consequences. First, while the officially rostered hours are shorter, the impact has been to make the workload to be handled in those shorter hours even more stressful. Second, the shorter hours have created an additional moral dilemma for junior doctors: do they leave work at the rostered time of 5.00 pm and be accused of slacking, or do they stay longer, either unpaid,[19] or fighting the hospital administration for paid overtime[20]? An annual Australian survey confirms that a significant proportion of junior doctors continue to experience adverse effects from their workloads and other pressures.[21]

Over these same decades, the pressures and stresses under which medical students, doctors in training and senior doctors study and work have also gradually increased.[22] These pressures include: heavy workloads and bullying, harassment, discrimination and racism for medical students and junior doctors;[23] for all doctors the obligation to keep up to date via compulsory continuing education with annual documentation of this to the medical regulator, the ever present threat of complaint to the medical regulator,[24] the threat of legal action for alleged negligence, the community's expectation that all illnesses are treatable and that all results of treatment are positive and free of complication, the guidelines that advise doctors to explicitly tell patients what went wrong when complications of treatment arise (a 76 page document!);[25] and the pressure to avoid allegations of over-servicing yet fearing not to miss a diagnosis. These pressures and others were documented yet again in recent Australian survey which noted 'the association between poor psychosocial working conditions and self-rated health in doctors'.[26]

In NSW in 2017, three junior doctors committed suicide within a short space of time. A distressed junior colleague sought to explain why this was happening and his thoughts were published in the *Sydney Morning Herald*. The stresses under which junior doctors now work are brought home with this short excerpt from his letter:

> Junior doctors are called the backbone of the medical profession, but at the same time it feels all too often as if we are its collective punching bag. We are told from day one we must always be extremely polite to nursing staff – whom I have witnessed belittling interns and residents without consequence. We are expected to work well beyond our rostered hours. We are told we must pay thousands of dollars for courses and exams and further our knowledge – but we are all too

often humiliated by our seniors in high-stress environments because, for all the things we know, we can never know enough.

When I think about all the things I have learnt at the end of my training, one stands out very clearly. There is something rotten inside the medical profession that has been festering for a long time. There is no realistic cure. The statistics about doctor suicide and mental health have been clear for years and yet our responses and solutions feel perfunctory at best and shameful at worst.[27]

The life of the new medical graduate now is undoubtedly more stressful than in the past. When I was a first- and second-year junior doctor in the 1960s, we lived in the hospital full-time. When we made mistakes we felt fully supported by the senior doctors (all serving on an honorary basis) and the nurses who guided us. The possibility that we might be reported to the medical board or be sued for negligence never entered our heads. While there must have been some stresses felt by some of our cohort, I am certain that we had it easy compared with the modern junior doctor. Looking back, I wonder if the fact of living in full-time, and the camaraderie and mutual support that was thereby engendered, made our lives less stressful and more enjoyable. The lighter workloads undoubtedly helped as well. In addition, doctors and nurses then had their own dining rooms, providing opportunities for informal but private de-briefing when things had not gone well.

As medical students, the major stressors for my cohort were the annual examinations. The university fees of most medical students were funded by Commonwealth government scholarships and there were no HECS debts to concern us. While some medical students supported themselves with part-time work, the hours worked were minimal compared with those worked by many of the current students.

For modern Australian medical students, the identified stresses include overload with new knowledge, repeated examinations and assessments, fear of not being able to cope after graduation, financial pressures, the experience of being humiliated or bullied by senior doctors, sexual harassment, and separation from sources of support when temporarily relocated to distant clinical teaching sites.[28]

These stresses translate into a significant incidence of burn-out, emotional exhaustion, anxiety, depression and suicidal ideation. As mentioned, burn-out has been reported in up to 50% of Australian medical students, depression in 18% and suicidal ideation in 10%. Fortunately with access to appropriate help, the vast majority of students are able to graduate and begin their careers as junior doctors. The need for access to 'appropriate' help was emphasised in a Canadian study that found that half the distressed medical students presented to a family doctor with physical symptoms and the real cause of their distress (emotional) was often overlooked initially. In my view, appropriate help for distressed medical students is best sought from a full-service doctors' health program, staffed by skilled and experienced doctors, which is independent of the parent medical school and free of charge to students and doctors (see Chapter 10).

Upon graduation, these new doctors face additional stresses. The stresses are particularly marked in the intern year and include coping with new responsibilities, handling death and dying, talking with the families of patients, and dealing with unpredictable workloads.[29] Some interns cope better than others but, for all, the capacity to cope is enhanced by supportive supervision. Just as for medical students, these pressures can lead to burn-out, anxiety, depression, suicidal ideation and suicide. Mental health concerns and suicidal ideation have been reported to be more frequent in junior doctors who are rostered to work unduly long hours.[30] These are not the only health and safety issues associated with long working hours and the related tiredness and sleep deprivation (see Chapter 12).

Once past the intern year, new stresses arise from even greater clinical responsibilities and the added pressures of choosing a specialty and competing for training places, as well as the need to study for demanding post-graduate examinations while working full-time. A recent survey of trainee specialist physicians in NSW linked stress, burn-out and depression with a pattern of insufficient sleep, insufficient holidays and insufficient exercise.[31] Worryingly some of these young doctors were already self-prescribing benzodiazepines. For junior doctors, seeking help is not easy as taking time off work may threaten their career prospects; even making an appointment to see a doctor can be difficult. Here again, doctors' health programs can come to their rescue by agreeing to see distressed junior doctors outside working hours.

When at their lowest from anxiety and depression, junior doctors need to be reassured that these responses to stress are normal for many young doctors and, in general, have not prevented doctors from progressing to an enjoyable and successful career in medicine. The qualification 'in general' is necessary because for a small number of doctors, these responses may be a pointer that they have chosen the wrong specialty or even the wrong profession. Expert counselling may be needed to guide these doctors in their next steps. For medical graduates, realising that one has chosen the wrong career can be a difficult, distressing and delayed process, taking many years in some instances.[32]

Let me describe in more detail the mental health issues that can bedevil doctors at any point in their careers and have the potential to end those careers and sometimes the doctors' lives. I will move from the least harmful to the most harmful problems, noting that the least harmful issue may be a harbinger of future more serious health issues and should not be minimised or ignored. I begin with the problem of burn-out.

Burn-out has been defined as '*a state of physical, emotional, and mental exhaustion that occurs as a result of intense involvement with people over long periods of time in situations that are emotionally demanding*'.[33] Symptoms vary and may include loss of job satisfaction, loss of motivation, cynicism, a sense of failure, and a reduced sense of personal accomplishment. The incidence of burn-out in medical students and in junior doctors has already been noted but the problem is not confined to doctors in training as even later in their careers, burn-out can afflict up to 20% of doctors in clinical practice.

Aside from the impact of burn-out on personal well-being, there are likely to be negative impacts on performance and career development as well as impacts on patient care by way of diminished empathy, prescribing errors, and other forms of suboptimal care.[34] Burn-out along with lack of sleep has been linked to needle-stick injuries and motor vehicle accidents (see Chapter 12).

While the issues in the work environment that contribute to burn-out can be similar to those that are thought to contribute to depression, it is held that burn-out does not itself lead to depressive illness. On the other hand, it is possible that some doctors who report being burnt-out may in fact be suffering from depression as doctors are not good at recognising depression in themselves.[35] There is no prescribed 'treatment' for burn-out but counselling, reassurance, and time away from work can all help. In addition, a number of techniques for minimising the feelings and effects of burn-out have been suggested including 'mindfulness' exercises, 'resilience' development, and regular exercise. In my view, while all these suggestions are laudable, I have to ask why the underlying stressors that lead to burn-out are usually ignored.

While working on this book, I read two media reports that indicated that some of those who manage our hospitals are blind and/or insensitive to the pressures they place on young doctors. One report was about the management of a public hospital that had ordered its doctors to complete their ward rounds by 10.30 am each day, an order issued without any consultation or any consideration of its impact on the quality of care.[36] The second report was of a hospital that threatened to punish junior doctors who briefly napped during quiet times while on night shifts.[37]

Personal approaches that might prevent the onset of burn-out include making time for regular exercise, leisure activities and hobbies; limiting working hours; and taking regular breaks and holidays. This advice flows from studies of the factors that seem to be associated with resilience in healthy doctors.[38]

Depressive illness is a much more serious problem than burn-out and carries greater stigma. The typical symptoms of depression include loss of enjoyment of life, low mood, sleep disturbance, poor concentration, lack of energy for even simple tasks, and in some people suicidal thoughts. For a few patients, depression presents mainly with somatic (physical) symptoms and in these patients the diagnosis may be unduly delayed. Depressive symptoms are often accompanied by symptoms of anxiety but, as anxiety is almost universal amongst medical students and doctors, and as, on their own, symptoms of anxiety are readily anticipated because of the pressures of medical practice, anxiety is not discussed separately in this book.

The impact of depressive illness is not to be taken lightly as every year in Australia young doctors in training and older doctors commit suicide. A report based on the National Coronial Information System showed that on average nine doctors die each year by their own hand and that 20% of these doctors are under the age of 35 years.[39] Psychiatrists and anaesthetists are believed to be at a higher risk of suicide than other doctors.[40] Women doctors are at higher risk of suicide than men for reasons not fully understood.[41] Some have postulated that the risk for women doctors is increased through having to not only cope with the intense pressures of clinical practice but also because they may take on a much larger share of home duties than do their male counterparts.[42]

It also needs to be appreciated that doctors are well able to conceal their depression and to keep functioning up to a point. This is hazardous for their patients and for themselves. Depression is also linked to diminished efficiency and clinical errors. Yet depression is generally treatable.

As mentioned previously, mentally unwell doctors are reluctant to seek help for reasons of stigma, embarrassment, and fear of being reported as possibly impaired. These factors especially apply to depressed doctors. In addition, the process of being suspended from practice and being under investigation as being potentially impaired has been claimed to have been the final trigger for many suicides of doctors in the UK. These claims led to an independent inquiry and an overhaul of the processes followed by the UK medical regulator.[43] A recent survey of unwell doctors who had been under investigation by the Australian medical regulator found that the processes were also stressful and, in many instances, doctors reported worsening health during those months.[44] Just as I was finalising the contents of this book, a newspaper reported that an expert panel has now advised the Australian medical regulator that the panel has identified 16 cases of suicide among healthcare practitioners who were under investigation by the regulator between 2018 and 2021.[45] The significance of this new finding and the related need for reform of the national regulatory scheme is taken up in Chapter 14.

Because of their medical knowledge and access to lethal drugs, doctors' attempts at suicide are more likely to succeed. Where they fail or where the suicide attempt was a 'cry for help', again stigma can be a barrier to support and understanding on return to work. For long periods of history, suicide was not only sinful in the eyes of many religions but in some countries it was illegal. The shame of suicide remains powerful even today. Family members feel uncomfortable explaining that a relative has died by suicide. One virtually never reads an obituary where death by suicide is overtly declared. These reactions may be relevant to the manner in which the medical profession responds to colleagues who are returning to work after a bout of depression and failed suicide.

So far, I have focussed on those common mental health problems that are tangibly related to the stresses of medical practice. Doctors and medical students may also experience mental health disorders such as psychosis or bipolar (manic-depressive) disorder, the origins of which are not directly related to the stresses of medical practice. When a severe mental illness with psychotic beliefs or mania occurs in a doctor it creates concerns for patient safety as the clinical judgement of the doctor-sufferer is often greatly impaired during an episode of illness. However, these illnesses are generally now successfully treated and most doctors with such illnesses are able, with support and supervision, to continue to work in the longer term. These doctors too experience stigmatisation and they too report insensitive attitudes from staff at the Australian medical regulator.[46]

Earlier I discussed the prevalence of self-prescribing by doctors, often involving the use of benzodiazepines, antidepressants and other psychoactive agents. The ready access to these drugs as well as to other drugs, particularly sedatives and narcotic pain killers, explains why abusive use of these drugs via self-administration is yet another hazard for doctors, especially those who are stressed and/or depressed. Unsurprisingly, drug abuse is commonly linked to depression and related disorders. However drug and alcohol abuse are problems for doctors in their own rights and thus I address them separately in the next chapter.

The misuse of legal and illegal drugs

Yet another health risk for doctors is their ready access to legal drugs (i.e. prescription medications). Misuse of prescription medications is a common problem among health professionals generally. However misuse is more frequent among doctors than for example among pharmacists and dentists and thus there must be additional factors involved beyond simply the matter of access. It has been estimated that one percent of doctors becomes dependent on prescription narcotics/opioids and that up to ten percent misuse other prescription drugs.

The biggest danger lies in the misuse of a prescription drug with addictive properties, such as opioids[1] and benzodiazepines.[2] This misuse is likely to lead to drug dependence with negative impacts on the health of the doctor and on the capacity of the doctor to practise medicine safely.

Typically, doctors who abuse drugs of addiction are adept at concealing their use until serious health issues or allegations of misconduct and poor performance arise. By the time of detection, their addiction is often severe. Fortunately access to professional help and treatment, often mandated by the medical regulator, can lead to good long-term outcomes, outcomes superior to those seen in persons addicted to 'street drugs' such as heroin. Good outcomes are not always the case as was seen some years ago in a cohort of NSW doctors who had lost their prescribing rights because of self-administration of opioids for non-medical purposes.[3] Of 79 doctors, ten had died and one third were not practising.

That same study emphasised that the most frequent means of detection was via community pharmacists who notified the relevant Health

Department authorities over concerns about doctors' prescribing and collecting of drugs. The most commonly used drug then was pethidine. However since that time, the ready avenue to access to pethidine has been closed off as pethidine no longer forms part of what was called 'the doctor's bag' of prescription items. As a result, pethidine misuse by doctors has decreased remarkably.

Another legal drug that can be abused by doctors is alcohol. Indeed it is the most frequently abused legal drug with reported incidences of alcohol abuse in doctors ranging from 10–17%.[4] The figure may be even higher as under-reporting via anonymous questionnaires is likely.[5] However it seems that the misuse of alcohol by doctors is of the same order as that of the general Australian population. Alcohol is used as a form of self-treatment for many issues by doctors. Its use is commonly linked to stress, burn-out, anxiety and depression.

An Australian survey of a large group of doctors from all areas of medical practice published in 2010 provides some additional insights into the risk factors linked to alcohol excess. In summary, heavier drinking was seen in male doctors, particularly those with Australian medical degrees, and in doctors exhibiting personality traits of neuroticism or extroversion.[6]

The dangers of legal drugs, which mostly involved opioids and benzodiazepines but also included alcohol, were borne out in a 2016 Australian study of the deaths of doctors by suicide or accidental overdose. Dr Jennifer Pilgrim and colleagues examined the National Coronial Information System over the years 2003 to 2013 and found records of drug-caused deaths of 404 health professionals including veterinarians.[7] Of the total, 254 were nurses and 73 were doctors. While the majority of the deaths were intentional, in one-third of the cases death was deemed to be unintentional (i.e. accidental), a surprising finding given that these professionals could be expected to be aware of the risk of overdose.

Among the 73 doctors, anaesthetists were over-represented. In most cases the drugs used had been obtained by theft at work or by self-prescription. The drugs detected at post-mortem included alcohol, anaesthetics (e.g. propofol), antidepressants, antipsychotics, benzodiazepines and opioids, often in various combinations. Very few of these doctors had been previously identified as users and all were employed at the time of their death, confirming that doctors are adept at concealing drug misuse, at least for a while. Concealment is possible because of access to very fine bore needles (so needle marks are unlikely to be detected) and because in the early phases of dependency, doctors are alert to the need to not work while drug-affected and the need to continue to work so that their access to drugs is not interrupted.

There are some groups of doctors at higher risk of prescription drug abuse. They include not only anaesthetists but also psychiatrists and emergency medicine specialists. However, all doctors practising clinical medicine are represented in the data so no group should regard itself as immune. The reasons for these differences among specialities are not clear. Background factors such as why any specialty was chosen may be more important than pressures of work and access to, and familiarity with, various classes of drugs.

Most doctors who misuse drugs have a diagnosable underlying mental health disorder in one or more of the categories described in the previous chapter but many have not sought professional help because of the barriers already noted. Additional stresses possibly contributing to seeking relief through drugs include marital disharmony, financial pressures and difficulties at work. It is likely that doctors who have both a mental health issue and are abusing prescription drugs find the barriers to accessing help even more intimidating.

Australian surveys, including the major one conducted by Beyond Blue, have reported that many healthy doctors regard both depression and the self-administration of medication by fellow doctors as evidence of personal weakness and unsuitability for the practice of medicine. There is scope here for better education of doctors on these matters.

Turning now to the use of 'recreational drugs' (illegal drugs) such as cocaine, marihuana and methamphetamines by medical students and doctors, it seems that this is increasing in Australia in parallel with their use by the broader community. Such practices are also potentially harmful to the future careers of these people as most of these drugs are addictive.[8] Users not only are exposing themselves to health risks but they may also be charged with criminal activity with consequences for their medical registration. The extent of their use was reflected in the statistics from the coronial survey of Pilgrim and colleagues where illicit drugs were involved in 9% of the 404 deaths in healthcare workers.[9]

If doctors do not die from their misuse of drugs, eventually (and sooner rather than later) those misusing drugs will come to attention. Occasionally one reads accounts from individual doctors who have contained their addiction within limits, evaded detection, and continued to practise medicine but such accounts are rare. Attention can be drawn to drug abuse from a number of sources: colleagues who observe unusual behaviour; workplace recognition of drugs being stolen; partners and families desperate for help; drink-driving charges; identification by pharmacists and drugs of dependence inspectors of suspicious prescribing; and last, deterioration in physical or mental health.

Treatment of the drug dependent doctor is similar to the treatment offered to other afflicted members of the community, i.e. detoxification, short-term or long-term drug replacement, supportive counselling, and participation in self-help groups such as Alcoholics Anonymous, but with some differences in the overall approach. First, withdrawal and detoxification are not possible without time away from work. Second, each doctor needs an individual monitoring plan (regular attendance for therapy, regular random screening for drug use) partly to ensure compliance but also vitally important if the doctor is to be declared safe to return to work. Third, because doctors see themselves as different from the average citizen (for the reasons outlined in Chapter 7), they derive more benefit from, and are more likely to actively participate in, a self-help group that has a membership limited to doctors.[10]

It is remarkably common for addicted doctors in treatment to relapse within the first twelve months.[11] This should not be seen as failure but is better regarded as a crucial learning experience for the drug dependent doctor. Thereafter relapses occur less frequently but monitoring and continued support is necessary for several years to ensure adequate protection of the community.

Depending upon the circumstances of the detection of the drug dependence, monitoring may be the task of the medical regulator but can also be undertaken by a properly equipped doctors' health program so long as the doctor is not impaired and thus not placing patients at risk. As I will discuss in next chapter, there are legitimate debates to be had over the competing roles of the medical regulator and doctors' health programs. The core issues are first, to clearly distinguish illness from impairment, and second, to find the best possible means of encouraging doctors in distress to come forward for help as early as possible. In addition it is vital that drug abuse be dealt with as a health issue and not as a misconduct issue.[12] Since the introduction of our national scheme for the regulation of the health professions in 2010, I believe Australia has gone backwards in regard to all of these issues.

10

Keeping doctors well: The value of doctors' health programs

In this chapter my frustrations at the intransigence of Australian health regulators[1] may become obvious to the reader. However, this story of the obstacles to adequate funding of programs intended to support better health amongst doctors needs to be told as fully and accurately as possible. My criticism is mostly of health and regulatory bureaucrats as I have encountered considerable support from a number of previous health ministers who deserve much praise. These I happily name.

The chapter focuses primarily on the Victorian Doctors Health Program.[2] I justify this focus on the grounds that it allows me to show that the Victorian program, although a first in Australia, was not original, being based on three to four decades of similar effective programs in Canada and the USA. It also helps to demonstrate what a well-funded program, one funded fully by the medical profession, can achieve and it enables me to document the inexplicable reluctance of the new Medical Board of Australia and the Australian Health Practitioner Regulation Agency from 2010 onwards to adequately support the Victorian program, by then ten years old and doing excellent work.

Sadly those responsible for the performance of the national regulator seem impervious to the reality that this is yet another reason for Australian doctors to neither trust nor respect the regulator. In addition, I suggest that my focus specifically on Victoria is justified by the apparent reluctance of other Australian jurisdictions to learn from the longstanding doctors' health programs of our North American colleagues. As a consequence, the limited health programs of most other Australian jurisdictions are, in my respectful view, not yet fully equipped for their task. Those jurisdictions are not alone in their tardiness as, in the UK, it was only in 2008 that the NHS in England established its comprehensive Practitioner Health Service.[3]

In Chapters 7, 8 and 9, I set out the causes of ill-health in doctors, the hesitation and reluctance of unwell doctors to seek early help, the obstacles to obtaining such help, and doctors' fear of the medical regulator. In this chapter I describe an effective means of dealing with these issues in a manner that should reassure the general community that unwell doctors are being assisted and assessed as early as possible and that the community is thereby protected. This chapter complements Chapter 11 which highlights one of the major obstacles to obtaining timely help, viz. the mandatory reporting requirement placed on treating doctors. In addition this chapter describes a means to overcome or reduce the obstacles to good care and at the same time meet the demands of even the most inflexible regulator. I also emphasise the important role that doctors' health programs can have in aiding recovered doctors to return to the medical workforce and in supporting the distressed families of unwell doctors. Apart from considerations of a general duty to assist persons in distress, getting unwell doctors healthy again and back to work represents a sensible response to the investment the community has made in training its doctors. As research has shown, the most caring of our doctors are among the most vulnerable to some of these health problems.

The concept of the Victorian Doctors' Health Program developed in the 1990's from a growing awareness within the Medical Practitioners Board of Victoria of the problem that no matter how 'user friendly' the Board made its impaired doctors pathway, the Board continued to see troubled doctors late in the course of their ill-health or their addiction. Sometimes this was too late for effective help. For example, in response to a request from the Medical Board in 1994, the Victorian Government amended the Medical Practice Act so that any doctor who was possibly unwell and impaired in her or his capacity to practise would now be managed individually and sensitively by a medical member of the Medical Practitioners Board. That member, usually the chair of the Board Committee dealing with health matters, was empowered to arrange an assessment by a relevant specialist whose selection was agreed to by the unwell doctor. The findings of that report were then discussed with the unwell doctor. If conditions, such as time away from work pending treatment, were acceptable to the unwell doctor, then the doctor was not required to appear in person before the Health Committee or a meeting of the full Board. Prior to this 1994 amendment to the Act, no such agreement regarding conditions being placed on a doctor's registration was legally binding without the unwell doctor being placed in the very stressful situation of appearing before a meeting of the full Board.

While the Board was confident that this change to the Medical Practice Act would help to reduce the incidence of late referrals, it was obvious within two or three years that the intimidatory effects of any dealings with the Medical Practitioners Board had been greatly underestimated. There had been no change in the pattern of referrals from colleagues or family members. The Board was also concerned that it had no powers to assist or direct unwell doctors towards the best available care and that there were no mechanisms in place to help doctors reintegrate into the workforce when their health was restored.

The Board then looked for a better approach and found it in North America where these issues had been recognised three or so decades earlier. There the American state medical boards and their counterparts in Canadian provinces had established physician health programs designed to support unwell doctors in a process that was clearly independent of the medical board yet sufficiently linked such that the medical boards would soon be made aware should doctors in the programs be practising against medical advice and thus placing patients at risk.

A word of warning about physician health programs in the USA is warranted at this point. The structures in place and the services offered vary widely among the US states. Some have their primary and even sole focus on doctors in trouble because of substance abuse and do not provide the breadth and depth of services offered by the Victorian Doctors' Health

Program. These differences need to be kept in mind when reviewing the extensive international literature on doctors' health programs. The Victorian program has more in common with its Canadian provincial counterparts.

The process of the establishment of the Victorian Doctors' Health Program occupied the years of 1998 and 1999. The process involved fruitful and positive negotiations with the Victorian Branch of the Australian Medical Association as well as strong support from successive Victorian health ministers, Mr Rob Knowles and Mr John Thwaites, from the opposite sides of politics. Their support was essential as the planned VDHP was to be funded via the annual fees that doctors paid to the Medical Practitioners Board for renewal of registration of doctors and this required an amendment to the Medical Practice Act. The end result was a program jointly owned by the Medical Practitioners Board and the Victorian Branch of the Australian Medical Association which opened in late 2000. From its opening, the VDHP had a written memorandum of understanding with the Medical Practitioners Board that spelt out, among many matters, the duty of VDHP to inform the Board should a doctor be practising against medical advice and possibly placing patients at risk.

Although the VDHP was part-owned by the Medical Practitioners Board, care was taken to make it clear that VDHP was completely separate from the Medical Board. The Medical Practitioners Board appointed half of the honorary directors of the board of VDHP, but those directors could not also be currently serving members of the Medical Practitioners Board. To further protect the confidentiality of doctors who sought the assistance of VDHP, the directors of VDHP were never provided with, and were forbidden to have access to, identifying information about the clients of VDHP.

In establishing the VDHP, what was not anticipated were the problems that arose from the joint ownership of VDHP, problems that came to a head when the Medical Practitioners Board of Victoria was replaced in 2010 by the Medical Board of Australia and its co-regulator of doctors, the Australian Health Practitioner Regulation Agency. More of that later.

Under its initial constitution, the objectives of VDHP were to:

- encourage the development of, and facilitate access to, optimal services for education and prevention, early intervention, treatment and rehabilitation,
- encourage and support research into the prevention and management of illness,
- facilitate early identification and intervention for those who are ill and at risk of becoming impaired,
- act as a referral and co-ordination service to enable access to appropriate support for participants and their families and
- ensure access to high quality rehabilitation and encourage re-training and re-entry to the workforce.

The early years of VDHP were very successful. Under the leadership of the first two medical directors, the program soon became the place where distressed doctors or their partners and concerned medical administrators turned for help. Even the Medical Practitioners Board directed clients to VDHP. Junior doctors and medical students in distress turned to it for independent help. Its value and effectiveness cannot be denied. It was filling a long unmet need.

VDHP does not provide direct care or treatment of sick doctors and medical students. A core role is to triage; i.e. to confidentially assess every new client in depth and then refer each person to the best available care. The service rapidly built up a directory of GPs and specialists with the expertise and willingness to assist. Every new client was helped to find their own GP if they did not have one – an almost universal finding. In selected cases, clients were invited to enter into a voluntary monitoring service that could include random urine testing for drug use, attendance at a peer support group, follow up contact from VDHP's clinical psychologist, and identification of a workplace mentor/supervisor on return to work.

Additionally, VDHP staff offered support to families and partners of unwell doctors, contributed extensively to the education of medical students and doctors about their health and well-being, conducted workshops to assist doctors in their complex role of caring for colleagues, and undertook and published research into the health of doctors. At a time when the annual renewal of registration fee was around $400, the cost of VDHP to the Medical Practitioners Board was approximately $25 per year from each registered doctor. For clients of VDHP, medical students and doctors alike, assessment and ongoing support from VDHP was free of charge.

Here is some data from those early years. In the years 2001–2008, 89 doctors with substance abuse problems signed voluntary monitoring service agreements. At the time of entry, a little over half of these doctors (47 or 53%) were not working, were suspended from practice, or were on sick leave, but within six months, 32 of this 47 were back at work. Of the participants followed up for five years or more since commencing the VDHP program, 81% (34 out of 42) remained well and in the workforce.[4] These results were well above international averages.

The numbers of doctors and medical students triaged rose from 42 in the first full year of operation (2001) to 148 in 2015. By then the total number of clients seen had risen to 1480, a number that represented approximately 7% of Victoria's doctors. Over those same 14 years, the proportion of junior doctors and medical students seeking help rose and the nature of their presenting problems changed. For example, in 2001, only one medical student was referred and 30 of the 42 doctors seen had substance abuse disorders. By 2015, only four new clients with substance abuse were seen. Of the 148 new attendees that year, 34 were medical students and 56 were doctors in training. Just over half of the entire group (87 attendees) were categorised as having a diagnosable mental illness while 68 were assessed as being unwell through stress and distress.

What was a concerning but also hopefully a positive development was that the services of VDHP were increasingly sought by medical students and by junior doctors in training. It was concerning that so many young people were stressed and distressed or experiencing mental ill-health. On the other hand, it was also possible that early intervention and provision of professional help might prevent more serious issues later and prevent loss of doctors from the workforce. Only time and research will establish if this is so. But the possibility is another reason for the existence of VDHP and similar services.

The support for VDHP from medical administrators of the hospitals in which junior doctors trained was immense. They quickly realised that access to the services of VDHP provided far greater guarantee of privacy and better access to care than could the counselling services offered via the hospitals' human resources departments. Medical school deans responded in a similar manner. While all universities offer support and counselling services for their students, the anonymity, independence and confidentiality of VDHP appealed to the medical school leaders. When the financial viability of VDHP was threatened by the new national scheme for the regulation of doctors after 2010, the medical schools were the first to come to the aid of VDHP. Later, the Victorian Health Department also came to the aid of VDHP because of VDHP's key role in supporting junior doctors in Victoria's public hospitals.

Thus the first ten years of the existence of VDHP were productive and positive. Then in 2010 a dark cloud appeared on the horizon in the form of the new national regulator for the medical profession. Whatever the intentions of governments, health ministers, and those who designed the new national scheme,[5] the end result has been a system of regulation of all the health professions that is not truly national, does not have the necessary trust of the health professions, has created a massive bureaucracy beyond the control of health ministers, and, in the context of this chapter, is inimical to the well-being of distressed doctors. Some of the failings of the national scheme for regulating doctors are also discussed in Chapters 11 and 14. Here I am focussing just on its impact on programs designed to keep doctors well.

The story of the survival of the VDHP is just one small element of this unfortunate development. And unfortunate it is because the national regulator has also failed to gain the trust of patients who lodge complaints against doctors and has been the repeated subject of inquiries by parliamentary committees. I do not for one moment seek to imply criticism of the conscientious people who staff the national scheme as I see them mostly as innocent participants in a badly designed system.

The task force that designed the new system was called the National

Registration and Accreditation Implementation Project. The task force's lack of understanding of the health problems of doctors and its failure to keep to its undertaking that the new national scheme would encompass the best of the state-based systems that it was to replace created several difficult years for VDHP. The first sign of trouble came when the initial draft of the new 'national law' was released for comment by the task force. Unbelievably the draft made no mention of supporting and funding health programs for doctors. With intense lobbying, this deficiency was corrected in the next draft, but somewhat begrudgingly as the wording left the matter of funding as an option (The National Law at section 35 (n) reads '*at the Board's discretion, to provide financial or other support for health programs for registered health practitioners and students*'). There seemed to be little possibility under the new legislation of VDHP receiving immediate continuation of the funds that were then being received from the soon to be abolished Medical Practitioners Board of Victoria.

With disaster looming, as the chair of the Board of VDHP, I sought an urgent meeting with the then Minister for Health in Victoria, Mr Daniel Andrews. It was the best meeting with a politician that I ever experienced. Mr Andrews was clearly well-briefed and extremely supportive. He gave VDHP (and its newer counterpart, the Victorian Nurses' Health Program) a guarantee of funding for the next three years. We at VDHP now felt comfortable that within three years, the new regulator, Australian Health Practitioner Regulation Agency (AHPRA), and the new Medical Board of Australia would have decided on a means to maintain the governance and funding of VDHP and to provide support for similar programs in all jurisdictions. How wrong we were.

The Medical Board of Australia refused to take on the role of co-owner of VDHP, leaving the Victorian Branch of the AMA with sole ownership. Worse than that, the Medical Board and AHPRA sat on their hands for the next three years and undertook no planning or consultation on doctors' health programs. Facing disaster, VDHP was only able to continue to function via generous temporary financial support from the then three Victorian medical schools, the Victorian Medical Benevolent Fund and the Victorian Medical Insurance Agency Ltd. And we lobbied the new Victorian Minister for Health, Dr David Davis. Like his predecessor, Dr Davis understood the value of the two Victorian programs and used his position on the COAG Health Council to have the Council direct the Medical Board of Australia to get on with its task.

The Medical Board of Australia's first step was to hire a consultant to survey the field, consult widely with stakeholders, and request submissions. The consultant's report advised the Board that the preferred model for a doctors' health program was the VDHP. It then took many more months for the Medical Board of Australia to decide how to proceed but eventually it entered into an agreement with the Federal AMA that the AMA would set up a national agency to distribute funds provided by the Medical Board to the various existing state and territory programs. That agency, established in 2015, is a subsidiary of the AMA and was initially given the name of Doctors' Health Services Pty Ltd. The new agency claimed that its task was 'to establish the first national health program for doctors and medical students in Australia'. This is somewhat of an exaggeration as it seems to me to simply be a better way of linking the existing state-based doctors' health advisory services and of publicising how to access them. Apart from the VDHP, there was no 'national health program'.

However, when funding was released, the Medical Board refused to fund a core element of VDHP's work, viz. its voluntary agreements with participants to be monitored and supported as they sought to recover and return to work. The shortfall in funding provided via Doctors' Health Services Pty Ltd represented a cut in the annual budget of VDHP of around 30%. The argument mounted by the Medical Board was that such voluntary agreements were akin to placing conditions on a doctor's registration and this was a task reserved for the Board. The argument of the Medical Board is specious as it ignores the common practice in the clinical areas of addiction medicine and psychiatry of seeking voluntary agreements as a means of encouraging and supporting patients in the difficult challenges they face. For example, these agreements can include an understanding that a breath alcohol test will be done at each visit or that, in private psychiatric practice, the patient will still be billed should the patient fail to keep an appointment. In addition, the Medical Board chose to ignore advice published in 1997 that 'the most successful models separate health procedures from disciplinary procedures as much as possible, and offer a confidential evaluation and treatment program'.[6]

Once again, VDHP was rescued, again by Mr Daniel Andrews, now the premier of Victoria. With his strong support, the Victorian Health Department, in recognition of the work that VDHP does in supporting distressed junior doctors, agreed to make up the funding shortfall on a permanent basis. Thus now at least in Victoria, distressed medical students and doctors have access to a program that is capable of fully meeting their needs.

So far, I have neglected to describe the services provided in the other Australian jurisdictions. Prior to the establishment of VDHP, New South Wales was leading the way in seeking to better support doctors in need. It had a Doctors Health Advisory Service, staffed by a number of volunteer doctors who could provide 24-hour telephone advice. The service had an office and a secretary and the service received some limited annual funding from the NSW Medical Board. In addition the NSW Medical Board had put considerable effort into making its pathway for assessing unwell doctors as user-friendly as possible. Those doctors who did access the NSW Board's pathway were generally grateful for the manner in which their health issue was handled. While to be deeply admired, the NSW approach in my view did not pay sufficient heed to the stigma attached when a doctor was referred to the Board.

Until 2000 Victoria also had a long-standing volunteer Doctors Health Advisory Service which was a telephone advice line staffed around the clock by two dedicated and experienced doctors, both nearing retirement. The Service had no office or other support. Similar situations applied in most other states and territories.

Now with funding coming from the Medical Board of Australia, via AHPRA, the way has been opened for every jurisdiction to strengthen and broaden the programs available to distressed doctors and medical students but progress across the nation has been uneven. Apart from South Australia which maintains a central GP clinic offering services dedicated to unwell doctors, the other states and territories provide only around the clock telephone advice for distressed doctors and medical students. Queensland's program contributes to education about doctors' health matters. Only Victoria provides formal triage, ongoing support and monitoring, and assistance with re-entering the workforce.

In 2020, the AMA's Doctors' Health Services Pty Ltd renamed itself 'Doctors for Doctors' and engaged a commercial entity to provide a 24 hour 'mental health advisory hot line' to supplement the advisory services it funds. The Doctors for Doctors' web site provides links to all those state and territory advisory services.[7] The link for Victoria is to the VDHP.

For completeness, I need to briefly mention that over the last two decades there has been a pleasing recognition amongst nearly all the key organisations involved in the training and continuing education of doctors that the incidence of distress and ill-health among doctors is alarming and that more needed to be done to reach out to distressed colleagues. Greater emphasis is now placed on education about the health of doctors at the student and postgraduate level, on encouraging doctors to have their own general practitioner, and on providing a range of means of peer support. A very incomplete list of such activities includes the peer support telephone services offered by many of the specialist medical colleges and similar services offered by state branches of the Australian Medical Association.

While improved education about health and well-being and ready access to peer support for students and doctors in distress are important developments, there will always remain a group of doctors whose ill-health needs more than just peer support. I suggest that the best source of that help and support can only come from a well-funded and comprehensive doctors' health program. As demonstrated in North America for five decades and in Victoria for over two decades, these services provide many advantages and benefits. An unwell doctor or unwell medical student is assured of confidentiality and a thorough initial assessment by a salaried doctor with the time, skills, experience, and knowledge to triage the unwell colleague to appropriate care. The program's doctors also have the capacity to sense when a doctor should not be working and also knowledge of the necessary networks to help doctors return to work. The program also provides a single readily accessible source of expert advice to which hospital administrators and medical school deans can turn. Such programs are also well-positioned to conduct research, publish their findings and be an educational resource. All of these attributes were identified and supported by a 2012 Canadian examination of doctors' health programs, an examination undertaken by an independent legal institute with a focus on public well-being and not on the interests of doctors.[8]

Doctors' health programs operate at a sensitive interface between the interests of community safety and the intense desire of some unwell or addicted doctors to keep working. As the stigma associated with notification of possible impairment to the medical regulator can only delay access to help, these programs are vital. However, every program requires good governance and good judgement of its staff in order to maintain the confidence of the community and the medical regulator. Clearly such systems cannot always be perfect[9] but equally I believe they remain the best option that society has to address the stresses that are necessarily associated with the provision of empathic health care.[10] A wise regulator would see the existence of health programs as part of the social contract that forms the basis of most medical regulatory schemes around the world.[11]

The telephone services offered by the voluntary doctors' health advisory services in jurisdictions other than Victoria and South Australia do not at present provide a similar range of services. The necessary change is not likely unless there emerges genuine leadership from the Medical Board of Australia with empathetic understanding of all the issues involved in helping unwell doctors. Based on past performance, optimism is not warranted.

11

The folly of mandatory reporting of unwell doctors

We seem to be living in an authoritarian age, whereby governments deem that problems are best solved by passing stricter laws. This appears to be the only reason why health ministers and the national medical regulator for over thirteen years have refused to recognise the folly of mandatory reporting of unwell doctors by their treating doctors. As the incoming President of the Royal Australian College of General Practitioners in 2017 accurately described this legal requirement, it is 'regulatory bullying' of sick doctors.[1] It is also self-defeating as the law deters unwell doctors from seeking help, drives the issue underground, and contributes to an increased risk that unwell and impaired doctors will continue to practise. Furthermore it undermines the trust that is essential in the doctor-patient relationship as it applies when the patient is a doctor. It also undermines the necessary trust that needs to be developed between the medical regulator and the medical profession.

Before explaining more fully why mandatory reporting is so unhelpful and potentially harmful for unwell doctors, I will briefly trace the history as to how the law arose and document the intransigence of state and federal health ministers, the national regulator (AHPRA) and the Medical Board of Australia. Prior to the establishment in 2010 of a single national medical board and single medical regulator, almost no state or territory government had legislation in place that called for mandatory notification by treating doctors of doctors under their care who were ill and possibly should not be practising medicine. No such legal obligation existed then in the eleven provinces of Canada, in the United Kingdom where the medical profession's regulator is the General Medical Council, nor in New Zealand. However, it was clearly understood in all these jurisdictions and was well understood here by our state and territory medical boards, and the doctors registered with them, that treating doctors were under an ethical and professional obligation to report any doctor who was practising medicine while impaired. The difference between a legal requirement and an ethical obligation is critical as it goes to the heart of the doctor-patient relationship when the patient is also a doctor as explained below.

In the consultation process which took place prior to the introduction of the 'national law' that established the new regulatory system for Australian doctors (which commenced in July 2010), the medical profession was seriously misled by the interim government agency that planned the new system. Doctors were reassured that the planners intended to maintain all the best aspects of the state-based medical board system and doctors were given an undertaking that annual registration fees under the new national system would be lower because of the anticipated efficiencies of a single system. They were sadly let down. Registration fees rose markedly, the system was not even truly a national one as New South Wales with over 30% of the nation's doctors opted out (followed not long after by Queensland), and the legislation included a new concept of mandatory reporting of unwell doctors by treating doctors. To make matters worse, as already discussed in Chapter 10, the first draft of the national law presented by the interim agency omitted any reference to funding of the existing doctors' health programs.

These problems with the national scheme were predictable, and indeed were predicted, but the planning group obstinately refused to heed the advice of people with knowledge and experience of regulating the medical profession. I for one identified many of these matters in a paper published in the *Medical Journal of Australia* in October 2009 some months before the final draft of the national law was agreed to by health ministers. Here are some extracts from that paper which was entitled '*National registration legislative proposals need more work and more time':* [2]

The Bill takes a complaints-focused approach, inappropriately regarding substandard performance and impairment as less serious categories of misconduct. This 'one size fits all' draft legislation has the potential to wind back important improvements to professional regulation implemented in Australia in the past 20 years.

From the viewpoint of the individual practitioner, most doctors have not opposed the proposed national registration system. Their reactions may have been different if the proposal had raised the likelihood (as the draft Bill B now does) of:

• a regressive change in how ill and possibly impaired doctors are managed;

• a mandatory reporting regime that threatens to make neighbour suspicious of neighbour;

• a significant increase in registration fees; and …

In regard to impairment, the draft legislation will set back improvements made in recent years that have resulted in earlier presentation of sick doctors and improved access to the best available help. It goes far beyond the modern legislation in most Australian jurisdictions in at least three ways: it extends the statutory reporting obligation to all doctors and not just treating doctors; it fails to separate illness from possible impairment; and it fails to identify that any possibly impaired doctor who agrees voluntarily to suspend practice is no longer a risk to the public and should not be reported to a medical board.

The approach to mandatory reporting of possible unprofessional conduct now proposed in sections 155 and 156 of Bill B, in combination with its definition of reportable conduct, is likely to create problems without any benefits. In their breadth, lack of specificity and bluntness of instrument, these sections are contrary to most of the current state and territory legislation.

Ever since those consultations conducted by the interim agency, I have struggled to understand why the medical profession's input was so studiously ignored. One possible contributing factor that I have entertained (but cannot prove) is that because NSW had opted out of the national scheme, some potentially strong voices were missing from the debates and the consultation process. In addition, any influence of the Australian Medical Association may have been weakened through the absence of voices from NSW, the most populous state with the largest proportion of the nation's doctors.

The legislation that was passed by the Queensland parliament in 2010 (the 'national law') and copied precisely in all other jurisdictions other than Western Australia contained all the flaws in relation to the ill-health of doctors that had been warned against. These flaws included the stigmatisation of ill-health by lumping impairment from illness in with other reportable forms of misconduct,[3] the use of wording that was in the past tense with the implication that even though an ill doctor was now voluntarily not practising, that illness still had to be reported to the regulator, and making the reporting mandatory for treating doctors.[4] Luckily for those doctors who resided in Western Australia, the local branch of the AMA was able to convince the Upper House of the WA Parliament to amend the WA version of the national law to exempt treating doctors from the mandatory reporting provisions (but not excuse treating doctors from their ethical and professional obligation).

Not only did the national law mandate such reporting, but the legislation insensitively and inappropriately placed this requirement immediately alongside, and forming part of, the mandatory reporting of allegations of sexual misconduct, practising while intoxicated, and professional misconduct in general. This misalignment sent the message to doctors that any illness that they may suffer was entirely their fault, a totally wrong but powerful message. In my view, this inappropriate conjoining may have blinkered the drafting team as to what was at stake. The conjoining still reverberates today in the legislation and in the guidelines issued by the regulator on how doctors are to interpret and apply the mandatory reporting components of the legislation. The legislation and interpretative guidance from the Medical Board of Australia fails to distinguish between impairment and mental illness whereas the two equate infrequently.

Three years later there was a missed opportunity to amend this faulty legislation. As previously agreed by the health ministers, an independent review of the new national regulatory scheme was undertaken by a consultant, Mr Kim Snowball, hand-picked by those same health ministers. Mr Snowball received numerous submissions on this particular issue, from the AMA, several medical colleges and many individual doctors. In his report he was unequivocal in his recommendation about mandatory reporting. On page 37 of his advice to the health ministers he observed that *'in Western Australia there is no legal requirement for a treating practitioner to make mandatory notification when a reasonable belief about misconduct or impairment is formed in the course of providing health services to a health practitioner or student. The intent of this approach is to not impinge on the treating practitioner – patient relationship.'* He went on to recommend that *'the National Law to be amended to reflect the same mandatory notification exemptions for treating practitioners established in the Western Australian law.'* Mr Snowball also noted that a similar exemption had already been introduced in Queensland.

The health ministers, now collectively called the COAG Health Council, did not accept Mr Snowball's recommendation and instead deferred any action 'pending further research'. The nature and findings of any such research were never published but three years later in 2017, the Australian Health Ministers' Advisory Council (AHMAC) on behalf of the COAG Health Council conducted a further consultation on mandatory reporting. Astonishingly for such a controversial matter, AHMAC gave only two weeks for receipt of submissions. I made a hurried submission which urged the adoption of WA exemption and also expressed disappointment that their *'discussion paper has not examined how the reporting of alleged impairment is handled in other countries. If this had been done, the paper could have advised readers that there is no mandatory requirement to report alleged impairment in the United Kingdom and could have drawn attention* to a very valuable independent analysis of the issues by the Alberta Health Law Institute in the Canadian province of Alberta.' I added 'There exists another simple legislative option which is to change the tense of the verb "has placed" to "will place" in the Section 140 of the national law as was advised several years ago.'

Not long after this, the health ministers announced that they had decided to maintain the mandatory reporting of ill-health but with a minor change to the wording of the legislation; viz. to alter the words 'risk of substantial harm' to read 'substantial risk of harm'. The ministers advised that they were of the opinion that this minor change, backed by an education campaign to be conducted by the Medical Board of Australia, should resolve the concerns expressed by the medical profession.

As Australia's unique 'national law' to regulate all the health professions is based on a law that was first passed by the Queensland Parliament, any amendments must first also be handled by that parliament. Thus the COAG Health Council's recommendation for this change to the national law was referred to back the Queensland government and parliament. Here the proposed changes to the law were subject to consideration and public consultation by the Health, Communities, Disability Services and Domestic and Family Violence Prevention Committee of the Queensland Parliament. This 'consideration' was in my view merely a charade. The report of the committee, made public in February 2019, drew attention to the fact that the majority of submissions the committee had received were opposed to mandatory reporting by treating doctors.[5] These well-argued submissions were ignored and the Committee advised Parliament to proceed with the legislative changes as proposed.

Surprisingly, one positive improvement in the national law did result from these four years of 'further research' by our health ministers. I refer to the small change where the past tense '*has placed*' was altered to read '*is placing the public at substantial risk of harm*'. This change is important as it means that any doctor whose health issue has led to a significant impairment, but where the doctor has voluntarily ceased to practice while seeking help, no longer needs to be notified to the regulator.

Here is the precise wording of the relevant section as the 'national law' now stands:

141B Mandatory notifications by treating practitioners of substantial risk of harm to public

(1) Subsection (2) applies to a registered health practitioner (the treating practitioner) who, in the course of providing a health service to another registered health practitioner (the second health practitioner), forms a reasonable belief that the second health practitioner is placing the public at substantial risk of harm by practising the profession –

    (a) while the practitioner has an impairment; or
    (b) while intoxicated by alcohol or drugs; or
    (c) in a way that constitutes a significant departure from accepted professional standards.

(2) The treating practitioner must, as soon as practicable after forming the reasonable belief, notify the National Agency of the second health practitioner's conduct that forms the basis of the reasonable belief.

[Note: See section 237 which provides protection from civil, criminal and administrative liability for persons who, in good faith, make a notification under this Law.]

(3) Subsection (4) applies to a registered health practitioner (also the treating practitioner) who, in the course of providing a health service to a student, forms a reasonable belief that the student has an impairment that, in the course of the student undertaking clinical training, may place the public at substantial risk of harm.

(4) The treating practitioner must, as soon as practicable after forming the reasonable belief, notify the National Agency of the student's impairment.

(5) In considering whether the public is being, or may be, placed at substantial risk of harm, the treating practitioner may consider the following matters relating to an impairment of the second health

practitioner or student –

(a) the nature, extent and severity of the impairment;
(b) the extent to which the second health practitioner or student
is taking, or is willing to take, steps to
manage the impairment;
(c) the extent to which the impairment can be managed with
appropriate treatment;
(d) any other matter the treating practitioner considers is relevant
to the risk of harm the impairment poses to the public.

(6) A contravention of subsection (2) or (4) by the treating
practitioner does not constitute an offence but may constitute
behaviour for which action may be taken under this Part.

The legislation above about mandatory reporting by treating doctors is supported by detailed guidance placed on the website of the Medical Board of Australia, so detailed that it makes for difficult reading.[6] One impression of these guidelines is that the Medical Board has concluded that the longer the guidelines are, the more helpful they will be! Another impression is that somewhere deep inside the Medical Board, there may reside an awareness that mandatory reporting is not the best way to protect the public as there is repeated emphasis on the point that 'substantial risk of harm is a <u>very high threshold</u> (my underlining) for reporting risk of harm to the public'. Treating doctors are then advised that this high threshold 'allows practitioner-patients to seek and have treatment for conditions without fearing a mandatory notification'. If these words are meant to reassure treating doctors, this may not succeed as shortly thereafter the guidelines read: 'There are consequences if you fail to make a mandatory notification when you have to. Although this is not a criminal offence under the National Law, your National Board may take regulatory action against you (such as, for example, a caution). It will consider all the circumstances before it decides whether to do so'. Even doctors with extensive experience in assessing the issue of impairment find these guidelines troublesome to interpret with confidence. Less confident doctors are likely to over report.

In debating any justifiable grounds for mandatory reporting by treating doctors, it was indeed unfortunate that our health ministers and their senior advisers (who constitute AHMAC) were not familiarised with the detailed report on this very issue that emerged from the province of Alberta in Canada in 2012. The report was entitled *'Physicians with Health Conditions: Law and Policy Reform to Protect the Public and Physician-Patients'* and came from the Health Law Institute of the Faculty of Law of the University of Alberta. It was prepared by an expert panel of five people drawn from across Canada; three academic lawyers, a religious sister with broad experience in public administration and a practising doctor who also has a PhD in medical ethics. This was not a group of doctors who could be accused of seeking to protect their own.

The panel's report makes for valuable reading. The panel was well aware of the need to seek the correct balance between the public's right to safe medical care and the rights of unwell doctors to be able to access high quality care without stigma, obstacle, or breach of privacy. They listed twelve separate known obstacles to access to care by doctors. They examined the reporting situation as it then stood throughout Canada, USA, UK, Norway, New Zealand and Australia. They pointed out that treating doctors may not have ready access to all the relevant information needed to justify a report of possible risk to the public. In addition, consistent with the importance of a positive doctor-patient relationship, the panel advised that the threshold for reporting a possibly impaired doctor needed to be higher for treating doctors than for co-workers or hospital administrators.

While some may see little difference between a legal obligation to report and an ethical duty to report, I firmly disagree. A legal obligation sends a different message to both the treating doctor and to the doctor-patient than does an ethical duty. This difference clearly impacted on doctors working within the Victorian Doctors' Health Program who in 2010 suddenly felt that instead of the previous trusting relationship with the state-based medical board, there was now a regulator that no longer trusted them. These doctors also observed a marked decrease in referrals to VDHP in the first year of the new national scheme. This drop off was attributed to unwell doctors' fear of being reported to AHPRA.

I have also been made aware of situations where 'fear of getting the mandatory duty wrong' may have led to inappropriate and harmful notifications. The worst such case involved inappropriate and unjustified reporting by a psychiatrist who should have known better as she was serving on one of the new state medical boards. That case also drew my attention to a serious flaw in the structure of the national regulatory scheme that makes mandatory reporting even more problematic.

The flaw relates to the division of responsibilities between AHPRA and the Medical Board of Australia. Most doctors assume that a notification of possible impairment will be sent to, and handled by, the Medical Board. However, the opposite is the case. The state branches of the Medical Board have no investigative staff and no responsibility for investigating any notification. The staff members responsible for assessing mandatory reports are employed by AHPRA and are only responsible to AHPRA. A notification may therefore be investigated by a person with no clinical background.[7] Without a clinical background, the subtleties of what constitutes a risk and how that risk can vary according to the area of medical practice will most likely be missed.

Any actions decided by a state Medical Board are based predominantly on the written output of those investigations. This situation undoubtedly contributed to a very unfair process endured by a doctor just home from a stay in hospital for treatment of severe depression. She was home unsupported and still suffering the after effects of her last ECT treatment when she was subjected to a telephone investigation by an AHPRA staff member. That staff member had no qualifications in mental health but used the outcome of the interview to inform the doctor that her registration was now suspended! The doctor had no plans to return to work until cleared to do so by her psychiatrist and her longstanding GP. This appalling process and outcome was accepted as satisfactory by the National Health Practitioner Ombudsman. I will refer to this case in more detail in Chapter 14.

I conclude the current chapter by restating and summarising the reasons why mandatory reporting is unwise, unnecessary and self-defeating.

As medical boards throughout the world have known for decades, unwell doctors are very inclined to delay seeking help for many reasons but primarily because of fear of stigmatisation and the risk to their income and professional status should they be reported to the medical regulator.[8] Those medical boards have repeatedly observed that unwell doctors, especially those with drug addiction, were seen very late in the development of their illnesses. Indeed, as discussed in Chapter 10, it was in recognition of these late presentations that doctors' health programs were first established.

In my view, and in the view of many others, mandatory reporting effectively undoes all the good work done in Australia between 1990 and 2010 to encourage unwell doctors to seek help. Not only does mandatory reporting increase the likelihood of late presentation but it threatens to undermine the trust that is essential to the doctor-patient relationship. It also unnecessarily raises the risk of unjustified or premature reporting by insecure treating doctors who may misunderstand or misinterpret the law, or who feel threatened by its consequences for a non-compliant treating doctor.[9] The distress and harm resulting from an inappropriate mandatory notification cannot be overestimated. Any delays in access to assistance increase both the risk to the community (from a doctor who should not be practising) and the risk to the doctors (through worsening health and in the case of mental ill-health, through suicide).[10]

12

Motor vehicle accidents and other impacts of sleep deprivation on doctors

Another source of danger for doctors is the impact of sleep deprivation. Every year in Australia it seems that young doctors are involved in motor vehicle accidents where sleep deprivation is a contributory factor, sometimes together with lack of experience in driving on rural roads. Some of these accidents result in injury or death of others or injury or death of the doctor-driver. As seen already in Chapter 3 which dealt with doctors who are assaulted or murdered, again there is no national or other register of these events. National statistics are kept for all fatal road accidents but they do not include the occupation of the driver.[1] The injuries and deaths of doctors are of course lamented but no lessons are learned. This needs to change.

In the absence of national data, I have to resort to anecdotes and they tend to have a familiar ring. One from Victoria is the story of a new graduate who was appointed as an intern to a Melbourne city hospital but for her first three months of work was seconded to work at the public hospital in a rural city that is a two-hour drive from Melbourne. As the young doctor resided in Melbourne, she drove home every second Friday evening to spend her weekend off at home. On one such evening she fell asleep at the wheel of her car and was dead on arrival at hospital. So here we have a young woman with no previous work experience to alert her to how sleep-deprived she was likely to be in her first few weeks of work. In addition it is likely that she was not experienced at driving long distances in rural Victoria. I doubt that these issues were considered when she was selected for this most stressful of intern rotations[2] or that she was counselled about the dangers of driving when deprived of sleep.

From South Australia comes a similar story, this one about the death early in 2022 of a newly graduated Adelaide doctor who was seconded to work at Port Augusta Hospital, a three-and-a-half-hour drive north of Adelaide. As at the time of writing, there is yet to be a coronial inquiry so whether this sad death was related to sleep-deprivation, inexperience with Australian country roads, or other factors is not known.

Medical students who are sent to rural locations for clinical experience are similarly at risk, especially those who are new to Australia or who have never driven on country roads. Dr David Iser, a general practitioner in Gippsland in Victoria, who was the co-ordinator of medical students rostered to local general practices in his area was alert to this risk. He also held an appointment to the regional South Gippsland Hospital at Foster and had learned of accidents that had befallen junior doctors rostered there. He was particularly struck by two such events. One was a young doctor who was unaware of the need for slower speeds on gravel roads and as a result rolled his car over on a bend. The second was a young doctor who had never seen a T-intersection and who drove his car across the intersection into an embankment.

These stories prompted Dr Iser to urge the medical school that was sending students to Gippsland to pay for a short course in rural driving to be attended before the students' secondment. The funding was provided only for a year and then the program lapsed. However, it is a practical example of what is possible to consider for the prevention of these predictable accidents.

These near-miss accidents and the two deaths mentioned above raise serious questions about why they happened and what parties should share some responsibility for them. Do not health departments and hospital managers and those who roster inexperienced junior doctors to work in distant hospitals without sufficient forethought to the dangers of sleep deprivation or lack of driving experience bear some responsibility? Do not the medical schools that send students to rural hospitals and rural medical practices (and insist that the students provide their own transport) also bear some responsibility?

'Drowsy drivers die' is a roadside warning familiar to most Australian drivers as are the campaigns of offering free coffee at highway stops during holiday times to encourage long distance drivers to take a rest break. The data about the impact of sleep deprivation on driving is extensive and generally well-known. Less well-known are the studies of the impact of long working hours of junior doctors on the risk of a motor vehicle accident. Even less well-known again are insurance company data from the UK showing that among 'at fault' insurance claims for motor vehicle accidents, health professionals filled nine of the ten top claimant groups. First and second in the list were surgeons and general practitioners; together they were 100 times more likely to make a claim than were clerical workers.[3] Experts who commented on this report attributed the findings to 'stress and tiredness' in those doctors.

The most valuable research data on the impact on the driving of junior doctors from working for very long periods without sleep comes from the USA. That nation has perhaps been the slowest to change the culture of expecting interns (first year medical graduates) to work continuously for unrealistic hours.[4] An important study was reported in the *New England Journal of Medicine* in 2005. It was a well-designed national study conducted over a 12-month period that attracted the participation of nearly 3000 interns across the USA.[5] The results showed that the longer unbroken shift that any intern worked, the greater was their risk of falling asleep at traffic lights or of being involved in a motor vehicle accident while driving home at the end of a shift. The risk was doubled after working an extended shift. 'Near miss' incidents were more than five times as likely as collisions. At that time in the USA 'most interns ... routinely worked more than 30 consecutive hours, a schedule that involved at least one night of acute sleep deprivation'.[6]

The effects of sleep deprivation on driving have also been documented under controlled circumstances with instruments used to measure signs of drowsiness and of inattention to the task of driving. In one such study, drivers who had been sleep-deprived for 29 hours were compared with drivers who had had eight hours sleep. The study also compared young drivers with older drivers. The differences were alarming with the sleep-deprived younger drivers having an eleven-fold greater incidence of 'near crash events'.[7] Surprisingly the effects on older drivers were less marked, for reasons that are not understood. Other research has shown that the ill-effects of sleep deprivation of seventeen hours are equivalent to the effects on driving with a blood alcohol level over 0.05%.[8]

In Australia, the work shift durations of new medical graduates[9] are shorter than in the USA but they can still be dangerously long. Since the mid-1990s, the Australian Medical Association (AMA), on behalf of its junior doctor membership, has led a campaign to protect junior doctors from the dangers of sleep deprivation. In 2000 the AMA issued guidelines on acceptable working hours which were updated in 2016. It has also conducted regular surveys of doctors' working hours, the most recent conducted in 2016 and published in 2017. While there had been a steady reduction in working hours between 2000 and 2011, the 2016 survey indicated that a plateau had been reached with 'one in two doctors (53 per cent) still working rosters that put them at significant and higher risk of fatigue to the extent that it could impair performance, and affect the health of the doctor and the safety of the patient'.[10] The average hours worked were 52.5 hours per week but some doctors were working 118 hours per week.[11] The longest shift worked without a break was 76 hours.

The data regarding average working hours of Australian junior doctors from the 2016 AMA survey are consistent with the findings of the larger survey conducted by Beyond Blue in 2013.[12] In this study, a quarter of the junior doctors were working over 55 hours per week. These long working hours have also been noted in other reports including in a submission from the NSW public hospitals to the Garling Inquiry which noted that full-time junior doctors worked an average of nearly 57 hours per week with 16% of these doctors working more than 70 hours per week. A more recent survey of physician trainees found that these junior doctors worked a mean of 53 hours per week, with 25% working over 65 hours per week.[13]

There are of course other dangers associated with sleep deprivation. It is not good for the mental health of doctors (see Chapter 8). It increases the risk of doctors harming themselves by a needle-stick injury (see Chapter 4). Importantly sleep deprivation in doctors also can place their patients at risk via its effect on doctors' cognitive function. With sleep deprivation comes slowing of mental processes, diminished alertness, diminished empathy, decreased mental and physical efficiency, and even impairment of memory. The impact of these effects on doctors' performance have been well-documented and include medication errors, errors in diagnosis, and mistakes made while undertaking surgery and other procedures. This should not be surprising as there is a vast literature from other fields on the links between workplace accidents and sleep-deprivation.[14] In most industries, protocols are in place to minimise these risks and to monitor and police the behaviour of workers, for their safety and the safety of others. Examples that immediately come to mind include airline pilots and interstate truck drivers – but not yet for junior doctors or surgeons!

Here is a summary of some of the research that has documented the impact of sleep deprivation on the clinical performance of doctors. One study closely observed the performance of junior doctors rostered to work in an intensive care unit.[15] With their consent, the doctors were randomly assigned to a standard roster or a roster modified to provide adequate periods of sleep between shifts. This was in the USA in 2003 so the standard roster involved being on duty continuously for 24 hours or more every third night. The modified roster was for shorter hours, no intern worked longer than a 16-hour shift and there were opportunities for adequate sleep. The study ran for 12 months. The interns were all closely supervised by more senior doctors and the errors reported in this study were usually detected and corrected before any harm resulted. The major finding was that the interns working the traditional extended shifts made 36% more medical errors than did the comparison group. The difference in errors were in relation to prescribing medications and in making diagnoses as there was no difference observed in errors in performing procedures. In a similar US study, also published in 2004, interns randomised to shorter hours on duty made 50% less attentional errors and were documented to get more sleep.[16]

Studies using surgical simulators used to train young surgeons have documented the effect of lack of sleep on the capacity to efficiently perform laparoscopic (keyhole) surgery. In a study from Denmark, surgeons who had been on call for 17 hours and had experienced a disturbed night of sleep performed significantly less well than expected.[17] A US study using the same simulator took a different approach assessing thirty-five surgical trainees on three occasions: when fully rested, after a night on-call that was uninterrupted by being called, and lastly after a busy night on call. When tested after the last situation, viz. a sleep-deprived night on call, trainees made more errors and took a longer time to complete the simulation.[18]

Most of the above findings and many similar observations have been known for nearly two decades but in Australia their impact has been muted to say the least. There are several possible explanations for this lack of impact. These explanations represent my opinion and do not have a strong evidence base.

First, it is likely that most doctors use rationalisation and denial to tell themselves that the effects of lack of sleep do not affect them personally. This would be consistent with the notion of invulnerability that develops subconsciously to protect every doctor from the stresses and emotions involved in practising medicine.

Second, there will undoubtedly be feelings of not wanting to 'let the side down' by insisting on obtaining adequate rest while colleagues continue to work. No doctor wants to be regarded by colleagues as unable to cope with the pressures of medical practice, a cultural attitude that will be difficult to alter.

Third, for doctors in training there are assumed negative effects on the gaining of experience that is claimed to result from shorter working shifts. This view is held by many older doctors. I am unaware of any research that substantiates this view. Perhaps shorter shifts with a greater emphasis on training and learning might be shown to be efficacious. While the former view persists, it will undoubtedly influence trainee doctors who will be sensitive to all the factors that impact on career opportunities.

Fourth, there are strongly arguable concerns about the lack of continuity of care for patients if their primary treating doctor is only available for eight hours out of twenty-four. For me, this is the only rational argument for having hospital medical officers work longer shifts and I frankly do not know the best answer to the dilemma. Even the most detailed 'handover' between shifts runs the risk of the information being misunderstood, forgotten, or ignored. The answer may lie in ensuring that all the doctors who are involved around a 24-hour clock, including at the weekends, are fully part of, and responsible to, a well-led team. This notion is expanded upon in Chapter 14. This approach will have cost implications, which leads me to my last point.

Fifth, for politicians and bureaucrats, any reduction in the paid working hours of junior doctors will have implications for the healthcare budget. Should any reader seek evidence of this, just recall the obstacles that junior doctors meet when genuine claims for payment for overtime are lodged. In considering the implications of all this, do not overlook the unrealistic expectations placed on public hospital managers to not overrun their budgets.

I will seek to address some of these issues in Chapter 14 but eventually they are matters for the community and taxpayer as much as they are for the medical profession.

Harassment, bullying and other sources of harm

Many of the sources of distress and potential harm to medical students and doctors described in this chapter have already been hinted at in earlier chapters. Each warrant more detailed examination in terms of prevalence, negative impacts, and steps that might be taken to prevent such happenings. Some of these stressors are common to all tertiary education institutions and many workplaces.

Sources and situations of distress and harm for future doctors commence during their years of education at medical school. Most readers will not be surprised at research findings that show that female medical students are often the target of sexual harassment and sexual advances from male colleagues, male teachers, and even male patients. They may be more surprised to learn that male medical students are also frequently subjected to harassment, humiliation and other stresses, mostly coming from their teachers. Unfortunately some of the evidence for this unacceptable situation comes from surveys of medical students in Australia and New Zealand. The situation is even more unfortunate as there is a belief that many medical students exposed to such conduct by their teachers will perpetuate similar practices when they in turn become teachers and mentors. Furthermore, it should be noted that most of the abusers are medically qualified university lecturers and senior clinical teachers. If any of these doctors behaved in these manners towards their patients, their medical registration would be at risk.

An early study came from an Australian medical school.[1] The researcher's survey had an 87% response rate, a remarkable figure that may reflect the seriousness of the issues addressed and the wishes of the medical students to draw attention to their situation. The specific issue addressed was the students' experiences of sexual harassment. Nearly 40% of the students reported some form of sexual harassment, the term including offensive body language, offensive comments, unwanted attention, unwanted invitations, unwelcome explicit propositions, physical advances and sexual bribery. Female students in particular encountered an unacceptable level of sexual harassment during medical training from fellow students, patients, faculty and doctor-teachers. For many students, these experiences negatively affected their learning opportunities. This was especially so where female students felt that they needed to avoid attending certain classes and clinical tuition sessions.

Another study from New Zealand a few years later looked at broader issues of student abuse.[2] In a survey of New Zealand's medical schools, 83% of 1660 students responded. As voluntary questionnaire surveys usually receive responses well below 50%, this response was also remarkable. Two-thirds of the students reported at least one adverse experience. The most common and the most distressing for the students was being humiliated or degraded by a teacher in front of other students. This was more likely to occur during the clinical training years and more likely again on surgical rotations, so once again the perpetrators were mostly doctors who hopefully would never treat their patients in such a manner.

The next most frequent yet also distressing experiences included unwanted sexual advances and unfair treatment on the basis of gender or race. Few of the students felt capable of 'brushing off' their experiences. Over half sought help and one sixth considered giving up the medical course. Even male students reported unwanted sexual advances from female nurses and some of the humiliation was delivered by senior nurses. These findings did not come as a surprise to the authors of the study as verbal abuse, humiliation, and sexual harassment of medical students had already been reported from other countries. Although not examined in the New Zealand study, those earlier studies had noted that these unhappy experiences were factors leading to anxiety, depression and alcohol misuse among medical students.

The above studies date back a couple of decades but more recent studies from countries with similar medical education systems show that the problems remain real and distressing. A 2023 report from the USA that used the euphemism of 'incivility' for this type of behaviour shows that sexual harassment, verbal and physical abuse, gender discrimination, bullying, and public humiliation are still rife, with all the predictable negative impacts on medical students equally prominent.[3]

From South Africa, also in 2023, came a remarkably similar report of frequent maltreatment of medical students by teaching staff at Stellenbosch University. Maltreatment included offensive gestures (75%), verbal abuse (65%) and discrimination (64%).[4] These experiences were linked to psychological distress which was more severe in female students.

Sexual harassment and humiliation (the latter presumably representing a 'teaching method' of some doctors and a few senior nurses) do not cease after medical students graduate as surveys of junior doctors have confirmed. A Canadian survey in 1996 reported that nine out of ten junior doctors had experienced sexual harassment taking forms that included sexist jokes, sexist teaching material and offensive body language.[5] A 2014 review of studies from multiple countries found that almost 60% of junior doctors had been exposed to at least one form of harassment or discrimination during their training.[6] The most common experience was verbal harassment while the most common source of harassment and discrimination were the senior consultants supervising their training. In Australia, the 2021 survey of junior doctors reported that 34% had experienced 'inexcusable' bullying, harassment, discrimination and racism,[7] a figure that was unaltered in the 2022 survey.[8]

While some of these reports came from other countries and the Canadian report was from almost another era, scandals that were reported in Australia commencing in 2015 relating to female surgical trainees have thrown more light on the seriousness of the specific issue of sexual harassment.

In 2015 a female surgeon in Sydney, Dr Gabrielle McMullin, made the ironic comment at a book launch attended by at least one journalist that '*What I tell my trainees is that, if you are approached for sex, probably the safest thing to do in terms of your career is to comply with the request*'.[9] Her remark was taken literally and a media frenzy resulted. A spokeswoman for the Royal Australasian College of Surgeons (also a practising surgeon) denied that there was a large problem. However, Dr McMullin's remark gave courage to a number of female surgeons and female trainee surgeons to go public with their experiences thereby forcing the RACS to establish a broad-based expert advisory committee to examine the issues. The committee found that 50% of the current College trainees had experienced bullying, sexual harassment or cultural discrimination. By November 2016 the RACS had issued its Diversity and Inclusion Plan aimed at encouraging more women into surgery and at achieving major changes in the experiences of its trainees. The College also committed to measuring and reporting responses to the plan and the actions that it called for.

In 2021 the College issued its first detailed report of progress with its plan. The report included its latest data on the prevalence of unacceptable behaviours.[10] The findings of the report are modestly encouraging although a number of barriers to progress were described including '*the surgical training environment remains an area of concern for reports of unacceptable behaviour. Contributing factors are systemic. They include the devolved structure of surgical training, which creates governance and accountability issues, workplace practices which create opportunities for unacceptable behaviours and lack of recognition and support for supervision in the workplace*'.

When compared with the survey conducted in 2015, it was disappointing that once again 50% of trainees reported exposure to unacceptable behaviours. These are now categorised by the College as discrimination, bullying and sexual harassment. On the positive side, there was a marked decrease in sexual propositioning so at least one message is getting through. This was counterbalanced by an increase in reporting of sexualised jokes and inappropriate remarks about appearances. Hopefully this increase represents increased reporting rather than a true increase in incidence.

The RACS has embarked on a long and difficult cultural journey which the other Australian medical colleges are watching closely and learning from. It may be decades before real changes can be claimed.

As part of its campaign to attract more women to commence training in surgery and keep them there, the RACS has been active in encouraging hospitals to provide part-time or shared training posts and assisting women trainees in other ways. The College provided financial support for a recent study of the obstacles that women surgeons face in their wish to be both mothers and surgeons.[11] Through the impact of graduate entry medical courses, the age of women now entering surgical training is more likely to clash with the time when most would also like to start a family.

The study combined an anonymous survey of College trainees and fellows with focus groups of trainees and senior surgeons. The survey drew 261 responders of which a third were men. Several obstacles facing women surgeons were noted but the major one was the lack of flexibility in surgical training programs to allow for breaks in training, part-time training, and adequate maternity leave (and paternity leave for men surgeons). Surgical trainees are routinely moved from hospital to hospital every six months and if the hospitals are long distances apart, the need for relocation creates enormous difficulties in terms of access to child-care and schooling. In addition, hospitals have been slow to provide crèches and facilities for breast-feeding. While hospital managers allow women surgical trainees to job-share, arrangements have to be made and agreed between two compatible trainees and are not the responsibility of the employer. The conclusion of the authors makes very clear that this too will be a long battle to change a prevailing culture for they wrote: *Many barriers to parenthood in surgery are created by rigid workplace and professional structures that are reflective of male-dominated historical norms. A willingness to be flexible, innovative and rethink models of training and employment is central to change.*

Once training is completed and doctors take senior and ultimate responsibility for the care of their patients, a new daily threat arises – the fear of complaint and/or litigation for negligence. Of all the stresses that doctors may be exposed to, the unfair publicity that surrounds actions for negligence is close to top of the list. It is typical that when a court action begins, the media coverage is based entirely on the allegations of the complainant. Any evidence on behalf of the doctor will not be presented until later and when it is, it is no longer newsworthy. All that the public hears is that negligence has been alleged against a doctor whose name is of course never suppressed. Even if the claimant wins damages, this cannot be taken as evidence of unprofessional conduct on the part of the doctor as medical errors are virtually never intentional.

Justice Michael Kirby described the issue aptly when he wrote:[12] *'Medical practitioners tend to see malpractice cases as involving a moral blight or stigma upon the practitioner concerned. From the point of view of the patient (and most lawyers) however, the issue is usually much more basic. It is whether a person who has suffered in some way as a result of medical or hospital procedures will be cast upon the genteel poverty of the social security system or be entitled to recover compensatory damages from the practitioner's insurance.'* There is a simple way of ensuring the rights of patients and reducing this stress on doctors and that is changing to a no-fault indemnity compensation system as now exists in many countries.[13] I will argue the case more fully in Chapter 14.

Complaints to the medical regulator can be equally stressful. As discussed in Chapter 8, a large number of suicides of doctors in the UK who were being investigated by the General Medical Council created great concern, led to an independent inquiry, and resulted in a revision of the processes used by the GMC. Until recently there has been no systematic examination searching for evidence of suicides occurring for this reason in Australia but one has now been completed.[14] That examination reported the suicide of sixteen doctors under investigation of the national regulator. The report reinforced my concern that the processes followed by the Australian equivalent of the GMC (the Australian Health Practitioner Regulation Agency) since its inception in 2010 have led to a widespread sense among doctors that AHPRA now treats any doctor who is the subject of a complaint as 'guilty until proven innocent'. The absence of personal experience of the pressures of medical practice among the AHPRA staff who investigate complaints undoubtedly aggravates the situation, as does the unduly long time taken to finalise complaints.

In addition, I sense that AHPRA staff tend equate illness with impairment and at times have treated drug misuse by distressed and very ill doctors as an unprofessional conduct or criminal issue rather than as a health issue. Again there are simple steps that should be taken by our health ministers to ensure a better balance between the necessary rights of patients to make complaints about the care they have received versus the harmful effects of insensitive handling of issues surrounding possible misconduct and possible impairment among medical practitioners.[15] These too are addressed in more detail in the next chapter.

14

What must be done

There are so many issues demanding attention that it is difficult to know where to start and how best to prioritise steps that might be taken to improve the lives of medical students and doctors and to reduce the risks and dangers they face. My foremost thought is that we should not seek to change the subconscious attitudes that doctors develop which are there for understandable and positive (and mostly protective) reasons and explanations. Nor should we assume that teaching medical students and junior doctors to be more resilient is the way to improve the pressured lives that they live. On this issue I concur with Dr Clare Gerada who wrote in 2021 that 'The fear I have is that resilience training is not about training to be resilient, but training to withstand abuse'.[1] Instead the focus must be on seeking improvements in the systems in which doctors are trained, the systems in which they work, and above all, improvements in the so-called 'national' system under which they are regulated.[2]

Improving the systems in which doctors are trained

Medical education has undergone major changes in the last 30–40 years. Many medical schools now accept only graduate entrants so students are older with larger educational debts and may have additional commitments including having a partner and children.[3] The graduate medical courses are crammed into four years with a curriculum that is crowded and intense. Emphasis is on self-directed learning as well as on gaining a wide exposure to clinical experiences outside our large traditional urban teaching hospitals. The latter can involve disruptive, expensive, and even dangerous travel to distant venues, usually involving travel at the student's expense.[4]

To date there is no evidence that graduate entry medical schools produce better doctors.[5] Many Australian medical schools have large enrolments such that educational experiences may be impersonal and students may feel unsupported. Senior clinicians' workloads make teaching and mentoring a demanding 'add on' responsibility that may not be being fully met. There is evidence that medical student well-being is enhanced through being part of a smaller medical school and through stability of the student group with which they are rostered to study and learn.

As we have seen, there are high levels of stress, burn-out, anxiety and depression among Australian medical students. In my view this data should not be ignored and should be the stimulus for a searching re-examination via a formal government-funded inquiry into not only the well-being of these students but also into the structure, aims and content of the medical course. The last such inquiry[6] was conducted nearly 40 years ago at a time when student well-being was not identified as a concern.

Since junior doctors experience even greater levels of distress, such an inquiry should also explore the transition between medical student and junior doctor life. The New Zealand practice of employing final year medical students as trainee or apprentice interns for part of the year (on a salary equivalent to 60% of that of an intern) should be carefully considered. Adopting this approach might require a return to a universal five-year medical course.

I am not a medical educationalist so I have no firm views as to what outcomes should be sought via such an inquiry. I do have a clear view that any inquiry must keep the well-being of today's students and tomorrow's doctors in front of mind.

Pending any changes to the medical student curriculum, it is vital that distressed or unwell medical students have unfettered access to independent, confidential and skilled assessment; effective support and counselling; and triage to appropriate ongoing care should that be required. For medical students at the four medical schools in Victoria this free service is already in place by way of the Victorian Doctors' Health Program. The Program is extensively accessed by medical students. This type of service needs to be available across the nation and I will return shortly as to how this could and should be achieved.

Improving the systems in which doctors work

As emphasised above, to focus on a single aspect of the well-being of junior doctors such as helping them to build resilience is inappropriate without at the same time seeking ways to improve the conditions under which these doctors work. Attention to working conditions will not only improve the lives of junior doctors but will also improve the care that they provide for patients.[7] Better working conditions may also reduce the number of young doctors who increasingly report that they are sorry that they chose a career in medicine.[8]

The working conditions of junior doctors in Australia must also therefore be the subject of a detailed well-funded nation-wide inquiry. This will necessarily involve not only examining hours of work but must include an examination of the level of support available to junior doctors rostered at nights and weekends when hospitals still try to function with what is a 'skeleton' medical staff. This may need a major re-think about how high quality around-the-clock medical care is delivered seven days a week to seriously ill patients in our large public hospitals.

The terms of reference of any inquiry should also address the complaints of bullying, sexual harassment and discrimination that are widely reported by doctors in training.

In Chapter 12, the tragic loss of lives of young doctors[9] in motor vehicle accidents when sent on rotation to work in regional hospitals was identified. Even before the critical issue of the working hours of junior doctors is dealt with, this risk deserves urgent attention. It must be addressed by hospital managers. Any small cost of preventative action will surely outweigh the human cost of losing the lives of some of our future doctors. One possible model of preventative action via driver education was described in Chapter 12. Another could be the provision of drivers for these at risk young doctors. If preventative measures are not seriously embraced, I hope that the families of young doctors who die in this manner take legal action to provoke the necessary reforms.

Any serious consideration of changing the working hours of junior doctors will be a more complex task than will be involved in seeking to improve the lot of medical students. For junior doctors there are three competing pressures: viz. safe working hours, safe and continuous patient care, and the need for trainee doctors to obtain adequate experience. Apart from some moves to roster junior doctors for shorter hours, the entire structure as to how medical care is delivered to hospital inpatients has never been the subject of a detailed review to my knowledge. Instead we are locked into a format that grew out of the era when junior doctors resided in the hospital and were available to provide continuous care around the clock. As a result we now have a situation whereby junior doctors are expected to care for allocated inpatients ('their patients') for 10–12 hours per day[10] from Monday to Friday while at nights and at weekends the care is provided by junior doctors who are unfamiliar with those patients and who are rarely well-supported.

One of the rationales for this system of provision of medical care is that hospitals are 'quieter' at nights and at weekends. It is true that elective surgery and elective procedures are in general not undertaken during these times but current inpatients do not suddenly become less sick after hours or on the weekends. Another rationale is the notion that trainee doctors learn more by staying in the wards and the operating theatres for longer hours. This shibboleth has never been tested. In my opinion it is equally possible (or even more likely) that well-rested junior doctors who work for shorter hours will learn more and make fewer mistakes than those who endure very long hours. In addition, well-rested doctors will find that studying for their postgraduate examinations will be less onerous and they will be more efficient in that study. And their mental health will be better.

In Australia there are no laws to regulate the hours that junior doctors work. The working hours depend on negotiated employment contracts and these vary from state to state. They usually provide that the maximum rostered hours are to be 80 per fortnight with a minimum of eight-hour breaks between shifts.[11] In the European Union there is now a directive that nobody should work for more than 48 hours per week and that at least 11 hours daily rest must be provided in any 24 hours. This has been put in place progressively since 1993. In any review of the hours of work of junior doctors in Australia, the benefits and drawbacks of the European directive in the healthcare arena should be examined. Those conducting any review must be cognisant of the repeated findings that unduly long working hours in junior doctors are strongly associated with the onset of depression and with suicidal ideation.[12]

Is there a way to achieve better working hours for junior doctors? Yes, there is more than one way. One way is to emulate the practices of nurses who generally work shifts of 8–9 hours with three shifts covering a full 24-hour day plus time for detailed handovers. Another approach could be to roster junior doctors for three or four 12-hour shifts per week, with a well-planned rotation system such that every junior doctor does an equal share of weekend and night work.[13] This approach is already used in intensive care units with an added paid half-hour to ensure a thorough handover between shifts. These junior doctors feel part of a well-coordinated team, a feeling unlikely to be shared by junior doctors rostered, unsupported, for night duty in the general wards of the hospital.

Both of the above approaches imply an increase in the number of junior doctors that any hospital employs. Employing additional interns has been done in the past.[14] This has budget implications but the cost of the salaries of junior doctors represents only a small fraction of any hospital's budget. Some of the increased cost may well be repaid through fewer adverse events and more efficient care with earlier discharge of patients, as well as improved well-being of those doctors. At the very least, these ideas deserve careful consideration and trialling.

Returning to the high levels of burn-out, stress and depression seen both in junior and older doctors, there are other matters that need to be addressed. Two constant themes are first, the difficulty that doctors have in recognising their need for help and, second, the intense stigma perceived with being unwell, especially if the illness is a mental one. Somehow all doctors need to accept that mental ill-health is a common human response to stress and must never be seen as evidence of weakness. Hopefully a day will come where a doctor putting his or her hand up for help will be admired rather than discouraged. In the meanwhile, there are two crucial actions needed in Australia that will lead to earlier and better access to care for distressed or unwell doctors.

The first is that the legal requirement of mandatory reporting by treating doctors to the medical regulator must be removed. It does not exist in Western Australia and as I explained in Chapter 11 it does more harm than good. I struggle to understand why our health ministers collectively have been so recalcitrant on this issue.[15]

The second is the desirability that the confidential services for distressed doctors in all jurisdictions beyond Victoria be bolstered to provide more extensive initial assessment and then ongoing support, including support for families, and support for re-entry to the workforce after periods spent away from work. One might hope that the leadership of the Medical Board of Australia would have the insight to recognise this need. After thirteen years of inaction I am not optimistic. Such bolstered confidential services must also be made available to all medical students.

While assaults that lead to serious injury or death of doctors are relatively uncommon, their impacts are devastating. It is interesting to observe that security in most government departments (including health departments), in our courts, and in our airports is vastly tighter than in our hospitals. Hospitals being institutions of care and of welcome to the sick and distressed are unlikely to embrace enhanced security at their entrances – although they did accept this as a defence against Covid-19.

The risk to medical and other staff of violent assault by patients or their relatives must be taken into consideration in the design of all new hospitals. This should include a separate entry and exit point for accredited staff who will not need screening. All other persons entering a hospital should at the very least be screened for lethal weapons. Designed into every new hospital, these controlled entry points will also be valuable for our next viral pandemic. In the meanwhile, there is a case for having security officers readily visible at the main entrance of every large hospital. Also security for staff who park off-site must not be over-looked. Some hospitals already offer security escorts to address this risk.

Never mentioned in the reports of increased violence against staff in the emergency departments of our public hospitals is the probable adverse impact of the otherwise desirable 'mainstreaming' of patients with mental ill-health.[16] One outcome has been that emergency departments of our public hospitals now are expected to cope with patients with serious psychiatric illnesses for which their resources and staff training are limited.

The matter of providing improved security in general practices and in the consulting offices of other medical specialists is more problematic. The suggestions offered by doctors with knowledge of general practice have included such advice as having a concealed duress alarm, always having two doors to any consulting room and where this is not possible, having the doctor seated closer to the single door.[17] Other suggestions have included steeper penalties for offenders[18]; education and advice for general practitioners about identifying and minimising risks; and enhanced identification of potential offenders. The great variation in the size of general practices and the profiles of their patients suggest to me that every practice needs to develop its own tailored security plan.[19]

Australia also needs better collection and monitoring of data regarding the various ways by which doctors and other health professionals can come to harm while doing their work. Occupational health and safety in the health care workforce has not been given a high priority in the past.[20] The scope of any data collection and the means by which this is arranged needs more expert advice than I can provide. In this book I have referred to the lack of centralised data collection on assaults on health professionals, accidents related to sleep deprivation, and harm to doctors and others from needle-stick and other injuries. My views on this lack of data collection and action are reinforced by the 2015 report of the Victorian auditor-general[21] on the subject of Occupational Violence Against Healthcare Workers which makes depressing reading. It concluded that '*Victorian healthcare workers face unnecessary – and preventable – levels of risk in regard to occupational violence. Despite all the audited agencies implementing improvements aimed at preventing and reducing occupational violence, the true extent of the problem in our health services and Ambulance Victoria is still unknown. Efforts to mitigate risks are incomplete and inconsistent. There is also limited evaluation of the effectiveness of controls in reducing and managing occupational violence'.*

The most obvious repository for centralised data on harm to the healthcare workforce is the Australian Institute of Health and Welfare, although should we ever copy the US model of a Centre for Disease Control, it too might have a role. The valuable National Coronial Information System already plays a substantial role but health ministers may wish to invite the NCIS and the state and territory coroners who contribute data to the system to carefully examine if there are readily remediable gaps in that data in relation to deaths of health professionals.

The receipt of allegations of medical negligence is another significant stressor for doctors.[22] This stressor can be readily avoided by the institution of a no-fault claim system as has existed in New Zealand since 1974. Most readers will be unaware that in 1975 the Whitlam government was poised to introduce legislation that would have copied the New Zealand system, a plan thwarted by the Governor-General's dismissal of Prime Minister Gough Whitlam. Fifty years of political inertia may be brief for some students of history but in my view this inertia is a tragedy not only for doctors but also for those patients who unavoidably are harmed by medical interventions and who struggle to be compensated. In the intervening years, no-fault schemes have been introduced in Sweden, Finland, Norway, Denmark, France and some American states.[23]

In a nutshell, the advantages of a no-fault indemnity scheme include faster, fairer and less random compensation for injured patients, less dilution of the benefits on legal costs, less distress for mostly competent doctors, more willingness of doctors to be open with patients when things go wrong, and more ready identification of possible adverse events and 'near-misses' by doctors along with their positive participation in processes aimed at reducing the occurrence of adverse events. In addition, through removing the threat of legal action, a reduction in defensive medicine and over-investigation should follow. Thus a no-fault scheme is the ultimate win-win situation (for injured patients and for stressed doctors). It is well past time for our politicians to act on this matter. Its introduction will cut across the interests of some lawyers and some medical specialists, two groups who derive much of their income from the fault-based system, so politicians will have to show courage in the face of well-funded opposition.

Reforming the system under which doctors are regulated

Since 2010, Australia's doctors along with fourteen other health professions have been regulated under a 'national scheme',[24] which is not truly national as half of Australia's doctors (those in NSW and Queensland) are regulated under state-based systems. The scheme, based around AHPRA and the Medical Board of Australia, is structurally faulty, has resulted in a massive dysfunctional bureaucracy that is distant from the health ministers to whom it theoretically reports, and has been the subject of four federal parliamentary inquiries and one state parliamentary inquiry (in Victoria). Without major change to its structure, I despair for the well-being of those doctors who reside in the four states (Vic, SA, WA and Tas) and the two territories (NT and ACT) who make up the other half of Australia's doctors.

I have written extensively on the faults of the scheme, many of which I predicted before the scheme was introduced.[25] Its only beneficial element is that we now have truly national registration with ready portability between jurisdictions. As the focus of this book, and in particular this chapter, is on the well-being of doctors, I will not try to spell out all the faults of the national scheme but instead will examine the faults that are associated with increased stress, anxiety and depression in doctors and which are inimical to the well-being of Australia's doctors, the vast majority of whom strive every day to do their best.

Non-medically qualified regulators whose only contact with the health-care system is via the complaints that they receive may become blind to the reality that nearly all doctors are indeed working conscientiously.

This view is supported by the content of two books written by experienced non-medically qualified regulators. The first was entitled 'The Trouble With Medicine' written by Merrilyn Walton and published by Allen & Unwin in 1998. This book was described by one medical reviewer as 'blood-boiling' on the basis that it failed to acknowledge that the vast majority of doctors were caring and competent. The second book was entitled 'The Good Doctor: What Patients Want', written by Ron Paterson and published by Auckland University Press in 2012. Paterson's book, while insightful, was misleadingly titled as it was primarily based on his exposure to 'bad doctors' during his ten years as the NZ Health and Disability Commissioner. I suspect that staff members at AHPRA have fallen into the same trap of sensing, incorrectly, that the instances of alleged misconduct they are asked to investigate represent the standards embraced by all doctors.

There is also a widespread lay misapprehension that allowing doctors appointed to Medical Boards to evaluate the performance of other doctors is a guarantee for leniency. Between 1992 and 2000, I had the experience of being joined on the Medical Practitioners Board of Victoria (at different times) by three legally qualified members and five community members.[26] Without exception, each told me that they joined the Board with this misapprehension and were surprised to find how 'tough' the Board was on doctors.

The vexed issue of mandatory reporting to the regulator of unwell doctors by their treating doctors has been discussed in depth in this book. The issue could be resolved quickly if the health ministers had the gumption to recognise that the Western Australian parliament got this right and if they had the honesty to admit that they were wrong to reject the strong advice that they received in 2014 from their own chosen consultant on this aspect of the scheme.[27]

A recent study of Australian doctors who have been subjected to the investigative arm of the national regulatory scheme helps me to point out one of the critical structural failings of the scheme.[28] Our national scheme has an unusual structure that is not easy to describe.[29] It consists of the Australian Health Practitioner Regulation Agency (AHPRA) and fifteen national boards (the Medical Board of Australia is the national board for doctors). The Medical Board describes its role as 'regulating Australia's medical practitioners; supported by AHPRA' but in reality AHPRA has all the money, most of the power, most of the staff and most of the strings.

Within AHPRA there is little medical professional input into the initial and subsequent investigation of complaints about doctors. If eventually a matter is referred by AHPRA for decision by the 'Medical Board', it is not the Medical Board of Australia that each doctor deals with as the national board is a 'hands-off' policy committee. Any decision taken by a 'Medical Board' based on the investigative findings of the staff of AHPRA will be made by what is effectively a sub-committee of the national board based in each of the six participating state and territory jurisdictions. Here at last resides medical professional expertise, supported by the views of community members, where most matters are adjudicated and where the more serious matters are referred on to a state-based disciplinary tribunal, chaired by a lawyer supported usually by at least two medical practitioners.

Among the staff at AHPRA, there seems to be little appreciation as to when one complaint is more serious than another.[30] Over the last 13 years a general feeling has been expressed within the medical profession that every complaint is handled by AHPRA as a 'guilty until proven otherwise' matter, with doctors having to prove their innocence. Having served on a state-based medical regulatory board for 19 years (the Medical Practitioners Board of Victoria from 1981 to 2000) I would not like to be serving on the current Medical Board of Australia (Victorian committee). My biggest concern would be having no knowledge of, or insight into, the skills and judgement capacities of the investigators employed by AHPRA on whose written reports my decisions would be based. As a Board member making truly crucial decisions about individual doctors, it would disturb my conscience that I had zero influence over the selection and ongoing performance of the staff on whose reports I was relying.

In my view it is this structural flaw that is at the heart of the continuing lack of confidence that doctors have in the national scheme. The flaw will never be repaired by tinkering. The best and simplest remedy will be achieved if every jurisdiction copies the example set by NSW and Queensland and returns to be independent of AHPRA, leaving the latter with the task of maintaining a national register of all health professionals. A Victorian parliamentary committee recommended precisely this step in 2014 but unfortunately for Victorian doctors the recommendation was not accepted. I wondered at the time why this was rejected and belatedly the realisation has come to me that Victoria has benefitted economically from Melbourne hosting the head office of AHPRA!

An additional structural flaw derives from the 'national law' which brackets health, performance and professional conduct within the same legal framework. This bracketing is singularly inappropriate for the reason hinted at earlier when I pointed out that no doctor ever deliberately sets out to become ill. This bracketing stigmatises health issues as equivalent to various categories of misconduct. This bracketing and the inability or unwillingness of AHPRA and the Medical Board of Australia to recognise the difference between illness and impairment to practise may be linked. The issue of ill-health and the associated possible impairment to safely practise medicine should have a separate section within the 'national law'. This view is supported by a UK doctor who has considerable experience in supporting unwell doctors.[31] A recent Australian study of a small number of unwell doctors whose cases came before disciplinary tribunals further affirms my view on this matter[32] as does the belated recognition by AHPRA that their processes for handling allegedly impaired doctors may be serving to aggravate the distress of those doctors and possibly contributing to suicides.[33]

I will leave the reader with just one example of the impact of this structural flaw. I am aware of this case because distressed doctors have frequently sought my advice and this is one such example. This case represents both the totally inappropriate handling by AHPRA of a general practitioner who suffered a relapse of a depressive illness and the lack of capacity of AHPRA and the Health Ombudsman to learn from AHPRA's mistakes. If the two agencies cannot learn from this case, why should any doctor trust the national scheme for regulating the medical profession?

The general practitioner had previously been unwell with bouts of depression but had always taken time off work when depressed. She strictly followed the advice of her own GP and her long-term treating psychiatrist to not practise while unwell. When she became unwell again, she arranged for her colleagues to cover her absence while she was admitted to hospital where her treatment included electro-convulsive therapy (ECT). While in hospital she came under the care of a different psychiatrist who happened also to be a member of the state branch of the Medical Board of Australia. Upon her discharge from hospital, that psychiatrist, without seeking advice from the patient's regular psychiatrist, notified AHPRA that the doctor was impaired and may seek to practise while unwell, a notification that was totally unjustified and very damaging to the doctor's well-being and potentially to her reputation.

The harm of this notification was increased when two investigative staff members from AHPRA (who lacked any knowledge or experience of mental health) conducted a telephone interview with the doctor the day after her discharge from hospital and at a time when she was still experiencing side effects of ECT given the day before. That interview came without warning and was conducted while the doctor was home alone and unsupported. She was told that her registration was from that day suspended – even though she had no intention to return to work until she had the all-clear from her own psychiatrist. The suspension was briefly publically announced on the website of the regulator.

The Medical Board maintained the doctor's suspension even after the receipt of favourable reports from her treating psychiatrist and her GP. It then became clear that three of the Board members who were party to that decision had undeclared conflicts of interest, primarily related to past working relationships. In addition, the whole saga was rendered even more stressful because of unacceptable delays in the handling of the notification. In seeking to complain as to how inappropriately she had been treated, the doctor first had to lodge her complaint with AHPRA. Not surprisingly, her complaint was deemed to have no foundation.

She then took the matter to the Health Ombudsman. Again there was an unacceptable delay. Astoundingly the Ombudsman, while acknowledging the undeclared conflicts of interest, chose to conclude that AHPRA and the Medical Board had followed their standard processes, had done nothing wrong, and that no action was required.[34] This doctor's experience reinforced my view of AHPRA being a bureaucracy that was beyond reach, unwilling to learn from experience and a danger to the mental well-being of the health professionals that it regulates. The regulatory system in Australia must be changed.

A revised regulatory system needs to acknowledge and respect the almost universal dedication of all health care workers to the best possible patient care. Although lay regulators may be reluctant to acknowledge the reality, the best judges of inadequate care are those health professionals who deliver good care.

Epilogue:
What lies ahead?

The rhetorical questions implied by the above title encompass two separate issues; viz. what can be done to improve the well-being and safety of Australia's doctors and what unknown risks lie ahead for our doctors? Neither question is simple to answer.

First what might be done to improve the lives of Australia's medical students, doctors-in-training and senior doctors (and all other health professionals, although I cannot speak for them)? My suggestions have been outlined in Chapter 14 but these are the views of one individual. There are many stakeholders who should be involved in this challenge. They include, in no particular order, our Parliaments and health ministers, health department officials and hospital senior managers, medical regulators, medical educators and elected leaders of the medical profession, especially the leaders of the Australian Medical Association.[1] A central challenge is whether to accept what was described in 2020 as the need to recognise medical practitioners 'as workers who, like others in health care, deserve basic rights and adequate conditions'.[2] That insightful article also pointed out that 'historical obstacles have allowed health care to subsist on the goodwill of its employees rather than reckoning with structural problems'. While written for an American context, there are close parallels with the situation for doctors in Australia.

Making improvements will not be easily achieved for at least two reasons. First, because in general doctors are well-paid, public sympathy for any complaints about working conditions will be difficult to generate. Second, I sense that because of the altruism and commitment to professionalism that most doctors exhibit, politicians, hospital managers and health care bureaucrats are generally inclined to ignore or minimise genuine concerns about the well-being of the medical workforce. The likelihood that responding positively to these concerns will impact negatively on the healthcare budget is undoubtedly a factor that will influence the thinking of decision makers. However, I would like to think that positive responses can only benefit all concerned, especially if this keeps more doctors healthy and in the workforce, and enhances patient care.

While improvement in working conditions will not be readily achieved, there is one action that our health ministers can act on immediately that will make a difference. I refer again to the need to repeal the mandatory reporting requirements placed on all treating doctors other than those practising in Western Australia. This single action will demonstrate goodwill and overnight will improve the lives of distressed doctors.

Any changes in response to these issues will also involve such matters as genuinely examining and documenting the occupational health issues experienced by doctors. If the health care system accepts this reality, i.e. to see the issues as ones of occupational health and safety, the medical profession also will need to admit the reality that the practice of medicine is stressful and that even the most resilient doctors are at risk of mental ill-health. Such an admission is contrary to the 'emotional armour' with which doctors are equipped. I am not optimistic that collectively the medical profession in Australia is yet ready for such an admission.

I have outlined a number of other desirable changes to, or re-examinations of, training and regulatory systems but the change about which I feel most strongly is to drastically correct the unfortunate experiment foisted on health professionals in the form of the 'national' scheme for the regulation of the health professions. It is not truly a national scheme, it has not won the trust of the community or of doctors, and its structure prevents the scheme from understanding what the issues are for each health profession that it regulates. This is also the reform that I feel most pessimistic about as the scheme has become a huge bureaucracy beyond the influence of health ministers. I can only hope that this book will open the eyes of, and foster understanding and courage on the part of, our state and territory health ministers.

The various personal risks that may lie ahead for doctors, nurses and other health professionals are a little easier to write about as they are unknown other than the certainty that viral pandemics will recur, perhaps naturally, perhaps via biological warfare. This may be in ten years or one hundred years. The next pandemic may or may not be particularly lethal. It would be encouraging to think that the recent experience of the Covid-19 pandemic will make all communities better prepared. I am not confident of this as I suspect that just as doctors see themselves as invulnerable so too do communities and that collectively our memories are short. I await with interest the findings of any government inquiry into what was learned from the Covid-19 pandemic. One finding of which we can be assured is that Australia's doctors, nurses and other healthcare and hospital workers did not shrink from the onerous responsibilities that they faced during the pandemic.

Finally, it is critical to state, as I did in the prologue, that despite the concerning themes covered in this book, people considering a career in medicine can be reassured that to practise medicine is an enormous privilege and that the majority of doctors find their careers to be very rewarding, even if also at times demanding and stressful, and very occasionally dangerous and deadly.

Notes

Prologue

1   Nava S, Tonelli R, Clini EM. An Italian sacrifice to the COVID-19 epidemic. European Respiratory Journal 2020; 55 (6): 2001445.

2   A needle-stick injury refers to a work-place accident whereby a healthcare worker suffers skin penetration with a needle or other sharp instrument that is or may be contaminated with the blood of a patient.

3   The first report came from the Manchester Infirmary in 1965. The outbreak of what was then known as 'serum hepatitis' preceded the identification of the virus now known as hepatitis B. Several doctors and nurses were seriously ill and one nurse died. In 1971 four staff members at the Western General Infirmary dialysis unit in Edinburgh died of hepatitis B.

4   Breen KJ. *So you want you want to be a doctor? A guide for prospective and current medical students in Australia.* (2nd ed). Australian Scholarly Publishing, 2020.

Chapter 1

1   The illness referred to as the plague is now known to be caused by a bacterium, formerly called Pasturella pestis but now called Yersinia pestis. The bacterium is carried by rats and transmitted to humans via flea bites.

2   https://en.wikipedia.org/wiki/Black_Death.

3   W G Bell. The Great Plague of London in 1665. Dodd Mead & Co Inc 1924 New York.

4   Huber SJ, Wynia MK. When pestilence prevails … physician responsibilities in epidemics. American Journal of Bioethics 2004; 4(1): 5–11.

5   Morris K N. Sir James Officer Brown: His contribution to the development of thoracic and cardiac surgery. *Australian and New Zealand Journal of Surgery* 1986; 56: 179–184.

6   The 2003 influenza pandemic known as 'swine flu' affected up to 1.4 billion people. https://en.wikipedia.org/wiki/2009_swine_flu_pandemic.

7   The high rate of mutation of the influenza virus lends itself to unpredictable variations in lethality, although the need for the virus to survive favours a trend to reduced lethality over time. https://theconversation.com/the-mysterious-disappearance-of-the-first-sars-virus-and-why-we-need-a-vaccine-for-the-current-one-but-didnt-for-the-other-137583.

8   https://www.ncbi.nlm.nih.gov/pmc/articles/PMC3329048/.

9   https://en.wikipedia.org/wiki/2002%E2%80%932004_SARS_outbreak_among_healthcare_workers.

10 https://en.wikipedia.org/wiki/List_of_medical_professionals_who_died_during_the_SARS_outbreak.

11 Australia did record six probable cases, all in visitors. https://www.who.int/publications/m/item/summary-of-probable-sars-cases-with-onset-of-illness-from-1-november-2002-to-31-july-2003.

12 https://en.wikipedia.org/wiki/COVID-19_pandemic_deaths.

13 https://www.who.int/news/item/20-10-2021-health-and-care-worker-deaths-during-covid-19.

14 https://www.bmj.com/covid-memorial.

15 https://www.ncbi.nlm.nih.gov/pmc/articles/PMC7598370/.

16 https://en.wikipedia.org/wiki/Ebola.

17 https://www.ncis.org.au/wp-content/uploads/2021/10/FS21-09-Intentional-self-harm-deaths-of-health-professionals-in-Australia.pdf.

18 Breen KJ, Cordner SMC and Thomson CJH. *Good Medical Practice: Professionalism, Ethics and Law.* 4th ed. Australian Medical Council, 2016.

19 Beyond Blue. National mental health survey of doctors and medical students. 2013.

20 During the writing of this book, my belief in this regard was reinforced by media coverage of an analysis of the suicides of 16 doctors who were under investigation by the medical regulator.

21 Sepkowitz K A, Leon Eisenberg L. Occupational Deaths among Healthcare Workers. Emerg Infect Dis 2005; 11(7): 1003–1008.

Chapter 2

1 For academic ethicists, I am happy to acknowledge that there is much sense in examining and understanding the ethical framework that a particular ethicist may be using, and that for ethicists, these frameworks are essential for progressing debate.

2 As should become clear from consideration of the entire content of this book, I am not seeking here to suggest that doctors do not have the right to eschew methods of medical care to which they hold conscientious objections.

3 In the 2016 edition of our text book *Good Medical Practice: Professionalism, Ethics and Law* on page 38 under the heading of altruism, with my co-authors we stated 'Altruism can be severely tested (and historically some in the profession have been found wanting) when doctors are expected to care for patients with infectious diseases that can be readily transmitted and can be fatal. Infection control methods and protective garb have reduced the risk of transmission, but altruistic doctors and other health-care workers still die of infections transmitted by patients. All those who choose to join the medical profession do so with this knowledge'. In the 2013 edition of *Ethics and Law for the Health Professions*, Dr Ian Kerridge and colleagues stated on page 906 'Health care workers have a duty to care for patients with infectious diseases, even if it is at a risk to themselves. This duty may conflict with other duties, and we may not all have the courage to undertake this duty but it is our duty nonetheless'.

4   With the following caveat: 'Physician conscientious objection to provision of any lawful medical interventions may only be exercised if the individual patient is not harmed or discriminated against and if the patient's health is not endangered'. https://www.wma.net/policies-post/wma-international-code-of-medical-ethics/.

5   https://www.ama.com.au/articles/code-ethics-2004-editorially-revised-2006-revised-2016.

6   The document is available at https://www.medicalboard.gov.au/Codes-Guidelines-Policies.aspx.

7   The Physician's Pledge is commonly recited at the graduation ceremonies of Australian doctors.

8   Lowns & Anor v Woods & Ors (1996) Aust Torts Reports 81–376.

9   Dekker v Medical Board of Australia (2014) WASCA 216.

10 Should the reader be interested in modern accounts of the impact of the plague, these two books are enlightening: Moote A L and Moote D C. The Great Plague: The story of London's most deadly year. Johns Hopkins University Press, Baltimore 2004 and Gottlieb R S. The Black Death. Natural and Human Disaster in Medieval Europe. Robert Hale Ltd, London, 1983.

11 Zuger A, Miles SH. Physicians, AIDS, and occupational risk: Historic traditions and ethical obligations. JAMA 1987; 258: 1924–1928.

12 W G Bell. The Great Plague of London in 1665. Dodd Mead & Co Inc. 1924 New York.

13 Zuger A and Miles SH. Physicians, AIDS, and occupational risk: Historic traditions and ethical obligations. JAMA 1987; 258: 1924–1928.

14 W G Bell. The Great Plague of London in 1665. Dodd Mead & Co Inc. 1924 New York.

15 Fox D M. The politics of physicians' responsibility in epidemics: a note on history. The Hastings Center Report 1988, vol. 18, (2).

16 Zuger A, Miles SH. Physicians, AIDS, and occupational risk: Historic traditions and ethical obligations. JAMA 1987; 258: 1924–1928.

17 https://en.wikipedia.org/wiki/Hippocratic_Oath.

18 In general, the term pestilence equates with the plague caused by Yersinia pestis but depending upon the circumstances can also refer to other disease pandemics and even to events such as widespread famine.

19 Zuger A, Miles SH. Physicians, AIDS, and occupational risk: Historic traditions and ethical obligations. JAMA 1987; 258: 1924–1928.

20 In 1988 the American Medical Association drafted a statement about the ethical duty to treat patients with HIV/AIDS but chose not to enforce the guidance. See Chapter 4.

21 https://www.ama-assn.org/delivering-care/ethics/what-physicians-duty-treat-during-pandemics.

22 https://www.ama.com.au/sites/default/files/2022-05/Position%20Statement%20on%20Ethical%20Considerations%20for%20Medical%20Practitioners%20in%20Disaster%20Response%20in%20Australia%202022.pdf.

23 https://www.professions.org.au/what-is-a-professional/.

24 Pellegrino E D. Medical ethics in an era of bioethics: Resetting the medical profession's compass. Theor Med Bioeth 2012; 33: 21–24.

25 https://www.cpso.on.ca/en/Physicians/Policies-Guidance/Practice-Guide.

26 Leonard PC. Imperturbability is not incompatible with clinical empathy. BMJ 2012; 345: e 4533.

27 Breen KJ, Cordner SM and Thomson CJH. Good Medical Practice: Professionalism, Ethics and Law. Australian Medical Council, 2016.

28 Pellegrino E D. Altruism, self-interest and medical ethics. JAMA 1987; 258: 1939–1940.

29 https://www.cpso.on.ca/en/Physicians/Policies-Guidance/Practice-Guide.

30 Dr Edmund Pellegrino describes this eloquently in his 1987 paper Altruism, self-interest and medical ethics. JAMA 1987; 258: 1939–40.

31 Universal or standard precautions refers to the use of protective garb, that may include double-gloving and wearing goggles or transparent face masks, when undertaking surgical or other invasive procedures on any patient. The precautions also cover the careful disposal of needles and other sharp pieces of equipment. They are designed to reduce the risk of transmission of blood-borne and air-borne diseases and involve the principle that every patient should be treated without discrimination.

32 There were similar thoughts expressed after the 2003 SARS epidemic: e.g. Ruderman C et al. On pandemics and the duty to care: whose duty? who cares? BMC Med Ethics. 2006; 7: E5 and Huber SJ, Wynia MK. When pestilence prevail … physician responsibilities in epidemics. American Journal of Bioethics 2004; 4(1): p 5–11.

33 https://erj.ersjournals.com/content/55/6/2001445 and https://www.bmj.com/covid-memorial.

34 Holly S et al. '"Will they just pack up and leave?" – attitudes and intended behaviour of hospital health care workers during an influenza pandemic.' BMC Health Serv Res 2009; 9: 30.

Chapter 3

1 Lorettu L, Alessandra M A N, Daga I et al. Six things to know about the homicides of doctors: a review of 30 years from Italy. BMC Public Health 2021; 21: 1318.

2 As I was undertaking final editing of this book, yet another violent attack, this time on a senior doctor working in an emergency department was reported in the media. https://www.abc.net.au/news/2023-04-10/senior-doctor-life-saved-after-stabbing-at-burnie-hospital/102205438.

3 https://onlinelibrary.wiley.com/doi/full/10.1046/j.1466-7657.2001.00094.x.

4 https://www.theage.com.au/national/victoria/hospital-workers-treated-like-punching-bags--one-attacked-every-hour-in-victoria-20161029-gsdnja.html.

5 Forrest LE, Herath PM, McRae IS, et al. A national survey of general practitioners' experiences of patient-initiated aggression in Australia. Med J Aust 2011; 194: 605–8.

6   Hills DJ, Joyce CM, Humphreys JS. A national study of workplace aggression in Australian clinical medical practice. Med J Aust 2012; 197: 336–340.

7   https://healthtimes.com.au/hub/patient-safety/45/news/aap/new-study-shows-methamphetamines-are-fuelling-violence-against-melbourne-hospital-staff/4696/.

8   https://en.wikipedia.org/wiki/Illicit_drug_use_in_Australia.

9   Lorettu L, Alessandra M A N, Daga I et al. Six things to know about the homicides of doctors: a review of 30 years from Italy. BMC Public Health 2021; 21: 1318.

10 Ibid.

11 Ibid.

12 https://www.smh.com.au/national/safety-plan-proposed-to-protect-doctors-20080629-2yv9.html.

13 https://www.smh.com.au/national/safety-plan-proposed-to-protect-doctors-20080629-2yv9.html.

14 This summary of the murder of Dr Tobin is based on many sources but for a full account, the book by Melissa Sweet, *Inside Madness: How One Woman's Passionate Drive to Reform the Mental Health System Ended in Tragedy*, Macmillan Australia, 2006 is recommended.

15 The day before, Australians had been shocked by the news of the terrorist bombings in Bali that killed 202 people including 88 Australians.

16 https://www.crikey.com.au/2009/05/18/how-i-found-out-a-killer-was-stalking-me/.

17 This summary is based on the sentencing report of the Supreme Court of Victoria: https://www.austlii.edu.au/cgi-bin/viewdoc/au/cases/vic/VSC/1999/225.html and a report in the Age newspaper: https://www.theage.com.au/national/victoria/you-ve-killed-me-can-i-please-phone-my-family-a-story-of-survival-20190409-p51cdv.html.

18 This account draws on these two items: https://theconversation.com/i-was-stabbed-14-times-at-the-hospital-where-i-work-i-survived-but-not-everyone-is-so-lucky-82824 and https://www.abc.net.au/news/2017-06-23/the-day-footscray-hospital-turned-into-a-battlefield/8526336.

19 This account is based primarily on the Supreme Court of Victoria's summation at sentencing. 2019 VSC 218.

20 https://www.abc.net.au/news/2008-03-26/man-unfit-to-stand-trial-over-murder-of-doctor/1083930.

21 https://www.theage.com.au/technology/in-harms-way-20070312-ge4eiw.html.

22 This is an abbreviated account of Kast's complex life and of the dreadful events of that fateful day. Fuller accounts can be found at: https://blogs.archives.qld.gov.au/2016/10/18/tragedy-at-wickham-terrace/ and https://medicalrepublic.com.au/murder-medical-patients-kill-doctors/12656 and https://brismania.com/day-137-medicos-murder-and-misdeeds/.

23 See R v Jolly, William Ernest [1993] Vic SC 371 (15 July 1993) and the Sydney Morning Herald https://www.smh.com.au/national/valiant-in-the-face-of-a-madman-who-had-shot-colleague-20090205-7z09.html.

24 Member of the Order of Australia.

25 https://en.wikipedia.org/wiki/AHS_Centaur.

26 Likeman R. *The Thousand Doors: The Australian Doctor at War Series*; vol 4. Halstead Publishing 2017.

27 https://www.mosmancollective.com/mosman-history-the-murder-of-heart-surgeon-dr-victor-chang-the-man-named-as-australian-of-the-century/.

28 https://www.theage.com.au/national/victoria/second-doctor-assaulted-in-a-week-after-sunshine-hospital-shift-20191119-p53bti.html.

Chapter 4

1 Ayas NT et al. Extended work duration and night work were associated with an increased risk of percutaneous injuries in this study population of physicians during their first year of clinical training. JAMA 2006; 296: 1055–1062.

2 In Australia in 2019 approximately 900 new cases were notified. It was estimated that there were around 29,000 people with HIV in Australia, most of whom were receiving antiviral treatment but it was also estimated that there could be 2600 people who were carrying the virus but were unaware of it. https://www.afao.org.au/about-hiv/hiv-in-austra.

3 Pneumocystis carinii has since been renamed pneumocystis jirovecii.

4 RNA testing refers to the capacity to detect ribonucleic acid specific to any known virus. It is the basis of measuring viral loads.

5 https://en.wikipedia.org/wiki/HIV/AIDS#Body_fluids.

6 Viral load refers to the amount of virus in an infected person's blood, expressed as the number of viral particles in each millilitre of blood. The lower the load, the less infectious is that person's blood.

7 The WHO estimated that by 2021, 40 million people had died of AIDS.

8 In 2021 the WHO reported 650,000 deaths from AIDS and about 38 million people worldwide living with HIV. https://en.wikipedia.org/wiki/HIV/AIDS.

9 https://www.hse.gov.uk/biosafety/healthcare.htm.

10 https://www.ncbi.nlm.nih.gov/pmc/articles/PMC3371777/.

11 See for example Zuger A and Miles SH. Physicians, AIDS, and occupational risk: Historic traditions and ethical obligations. JAMA 1987; 258: 1924–1928 and Daniels N. Duty to treat or right to refuse? The Hastings Center Report March-April 1991, vol 21, issue 2.

12 A notable exception to a lack of community consultation occurred in 2009 when the Australian Medical Council on behalf of the state and territory medical boards developed the code of conduct known as *Good Medical Practice: a code of conduct for doctors in Australia*. In the process of developing the Code there was extensive community consultation. The Code was adopted by the new Medical Board of Australia in 2010.

13 Surveys of US doctors showed that up to half believed that they had no obligation to treat people who had HIV.

14 Pellegrino E D. Altruism and exposure to risk. JAMA 1987; 258: 1939–1940.

15 The Australian general practitioners who took on this work deserve great admiration. This retrospective description of their experiences explains how difficult the work was – https://www.racgp.org.au/afp/2013/october/surviving-an-epidemic.

16 Physician/researcher, the late Dr David Cooper, inspirationally led the outstanding work at St Vincent's Hospital in Sydney. https://www.news.com.au/technology/science/human-body/the-man-who-diagnosed-australias-first-hiv-case-dies/news-story/cea425e66bbdf3a78fa383d814a0bbfd.

17 https://www.cdc.gov/infectioncontrol/basics/standard-precautions.html.

18 A 2004 study from a UK hospital found that only 50% of needle-stick events were reported by staff and for doctors the reporting rate was even lower. https://pubmed.ncbi.nlm.nih.gov/15229257/.

19 Death of surgeon from AIDS raises controversy. BMJ 1994; 309: 222.

20 https://www.health.gov.au/sites/default/files/documents/2020/03/cdna-guidance-on-classification-of-exposure-prone-and-non-exposure-prone-procedures-in-australia-2017.pdf.

21 Australian national guidelines for the management of healthcare workers living with blood borne viruses and healthcare workers who perform exposure prone procedures at risk of exposure to blood borne viruses. https://www.health.gov.au/resources/publications/cdna-national-guidelines-healthcare-workers-living-with-blood-borne-viruses-perform-exposure-prone-procedures-at-risk-of-exposure-to-blood-borne-viruses?language=en.

22 Guidelines – Registered health practitioners and students in relation to blood-borne viruses https://www.medicalboard.gov.au/Codes-Guidelines-Policies.aspx.

23 In 1992 it was reported that a dentist in the USA was found to have transmitted HIV to six patients and in 1999 it was reported that an orthopaedic surgeon in France probably transmitted HIV to one patient. Lot F, Jean-Christophe Séguier J-C, Fégueux S. et al. Probable Transmission of HIV from an Orthopaedic Surgeon to a Patient in France. Annals of Internal Medicine 1999; 130(1): 1–6.

24 https://www.tampabay.com/archive/1990/07/07/doctors-british-sailor-died-of-aids-in-1959/.

25 https://www.ncbi.nlm.nih.gov/pmc/articles/PMC6496330/ This account pays credit to Australian researchers at Fairfield Infectious Diseases Hospital in Melbourne for their pursuit of the hepatitis A virus.

26 Breen KJ. *So you want to be a doctor: A guide for prospective and current medical students in Australia.* 2nd ed. Australian Scholarly Publishing, 2020, p 106.

27 Incubation period refers to the number of days between exposure to an infectious agent and the development of illness.

28 This refers to research conducted at the infamous Willowbrook Institute for intellectually handicapped children in New York and in US prisons.

29 https://www.ncbi.nlm.nih.gov/pmc/articles/PMC3729363/ This article provides a detailed history of advances in understanding hepatitis B made over the last fifty years.

30 These guidelines extend to all other infectious diseases that health care workers might spread to patients. They are updated regularly and can be found here https://www.health.gov.au/resources/collections/cdna-national-guidelines-for-healthcare-workers-on-managing-bloodborne-viruses?language=en.

31 Although the virus has not been cultured, researchers have been able to clone a version of the virus in the laboratory based on the precise knowledge of its genome.

32 https://www.theage.com.au/national/victoria/anaesthetist-who-infected-55-women-with-hep-c-to-challenge-conviction-20181009-p508oz.html.

33 McCaughan GW, Munn S R. Liver transplantation in Australia and New Zealand. Liver Transplantation 2016; 22 (6): 830–838.

34 Watson KJR. Surgeon, test (and heal) thyself: sharps injuries and hepatitis C risk. Med J Aust 2004; vol 181: 366–367.

35 https://www.nps.org.au/australian-prescriber/articles/needle-stick-injuries-in-primary-care.

Chapter 5

1   J M Barry. The Great Influenza. Penguin Books 2005.

2   Cytokine storm refers to the release of chemicals within the body that can provoke life-threatening over-activation of the body's defence systems. The reaction can be triggered by a number of stimuli of which infection is the most common.

3   Such generalised bleeding would now most likely be attributed to 'disseminated intravascular coagulation' (DIC). Closely related to cytokine storm, DIC is a rare but serious condition that causes abnormal blood clotting followed by depletion of clotting agents and hence generalised bleeding. Again, its most common precipitant is overwhelming infection, viral or bacterial.

4   https://en.wikipedia.org/wiki/Spanish_flu.

5   https://www.theguardian.com/world/2020/apr/05/nurses-fell-like-ninepins-death-and-bravery-in-the-1918-flu-pandemic.

6   https://en.wikipedia.org/wiki/1957%E2%80%931958_influenza_pandemic.

7   https://en.wikipedia.org/wiki/Hong_Kong_flu.

8   https://en.wikipedia.org/wiki/1977_Russian_flu.

9   https://en.wikipedia.org/wiki/2009_swine_flu_pandemic.

10 https://www.who.int/news-room/fact-sheets/detail/influenza-(seasonal).

11 Bull A L et al. Influenza vaccine coverage among health care workers in Victorian public hospitals. Med J Aust 2007; 186(4): 185–6.

12 Taubenberger JK et al. Reconstruction of the 1918 Influenza Virus: Unexpected Rewards from the Past. American Society of Microbiology Journals mBio 2012 Sept 11, vol. 3, No. 5 DOI: https://doi.org/10.1128/mBio.00201-12.

13 https://www.thesaturdaypaper.com.au/opinion/topic/2022/12/17/what-we-got-wrong-about-covid-19.

14 https://news.un.org/en/story/2003/03/63422.

15 The first inquiry was conducted by Justice Archie Campbell for the provincial government of Ontario – http://www.archives.gov.on.ca/en/e_records/sars/report/index.html The second Canadian inquiry was a nation-wide one – https://www.canada.ca/content/dam/phac-aspc/migration/phac-aspc/publicat/sars-sras/pdf/sars-e.pdf.

16 This quotation is from the Ontario inquiry conducted by Justice Archie Campbell – http://www.archives.gov.on.ca/en/e_records/sars/report/index.html.

17 https://en.wikipedia.org/wiki/List_of_medical_professionals_who_died_during_the_SARS_outbreak.

18 https://www.ncbi.nlm.nih.gov/pmc/articles/PMC3371777/.

19 https://en.wikipedia.org/wiki/SARS.

20 https://en.wikipedia.org/wiki/MERS.

21 https://www.aihw.gov.au/reports/burden-of-disease/the-first-year-of-covid-19-in-australia/summary.

22 Muhi S, Irving LB, Buising KL. COVID-19 in Australian health care workers: early experience of the Royal Melbourne Hospital emphasises the importance of community acquisition. Med J Aust 2020; 213(1): 44–44.

23 Several studies have been published. This is a good example: Hunter R, Willis K, Smallwood N. The workplace and psychosocial experiences of Australian junior doctors during the COVID-19 pandemic. Intern Med J 2022; 52(5): 745–754.

24 Presenteeism, invented as a term opposite to absenteeism, means working when unwell. Hunter R, Willis K, Smallwood N. The workplace and psychosocial experiences of Australian junior doctors during the COVID-19 pandemic. Intern Med J 2022; 52(5): 745–754.

Chapter 6

1 Bacteria are larger than viruses, can be seen by ordinary microscopy, can be grown in the laboratory and can be treated with antibiotic drugs. Viruses are much smaller, cannot be grown outside a living host and do not respond to the administration of antibiotics.

2 Beyond the emerging or re-emerging infectious diseases mentioned in this chapter, there are many other diseases that are still the cause of epidemics in developing countries, with consequent serious morbidity and mortality. Examples include cholera, measles, meningitis and poliomyelitis. These too can place healthcare workers at risk.

3 The traditional funerary rites in Africa often involve families washing and kissing the body of the deceased. For the Ebola virus this puts family members at serious risk of transmission of the virus. Cordner S, Bouwer H, Tidball-Binz M. The Ebola epidemic in Liberia and managing the dead – A future role for Humanitarian Forensic Action? Forensic Science International 2017; 279: 302–309.

4 Jacob, S.T., Crozier, I., Fischer, W.A. et al. Ebola virus disease. Nat Rev Dis Primers 6, 13 (2020).

5 https://en.wikipedia.org/wiki/Ebola.

6 Green A. Obituary. Remembering health workers who died from Ebola in 2014. Lancet 2014; 384: 2210–2206.

7 Climate change may also explain the arrival of Japanese B encephalitis which had never been endemic on the Australian mainland until the first locally acquired cases were notified in 2021/22.

8 https://www.who.int/health-topics/marburg-virus-disease#tab=tab_1.

9 https://www.cdc.gov/vhf/hendra/index.html.

10 https://www.health.nsw.gov.au/Infectious/factsheets/Pages/hendra_virus.aspx.

11 The test is called the tuberculin or Mantoux test and involves injecting a minute amount of sterile extract of the tubercle bacillus into the skin of the forearm. Persons harbouring the TB bacillus will mount an immune reaction with swelling appearing over the next 2–4 days.

12 Preventing tuberculosis infection and disease among healthcare workers. https://www.google.com/url?sa=t&rct=j&q=&esrc=s&s ource=web&cd=&ved=2ahUKEwjItdjX35j9AhWd-TgGHUR7D gkQFnoECDYQAQ&url=https%3A%2F%2Fwww.thermh.org. au%2Ffile%2F3598&usg=AOvVaw3NK4dxh9tm9iDeW1PXXzh3.

Chapter 7

1 Frank E, Brogan DJ, Mokdad AH et al. Health-related behaviours of women physicians vs other women in the United States. Arch Intern Med 1998; 158: 342–34.

2 This despite the injunction in the AMA's Code of Ethics at 3.1.4 'Take responsibility for your own health and well-being including having your own general practitioner'. https://www.ama.com.au/articles/code-ethics-2004-editorially-revised-2006-revised-2016.

3 Kay MP, Mitchell GK, Del Mar CB. Doctors do not adequately look after their own physical health. Med J Aust 2004; 181: 368–370.

4 Self-prescribing can range from over-the counter medications to antibiotics and anti-inflammatory drugs and to mood-altering drugs or drugs of dependence.

5 Kay, M.P., Mitchell, G.K. and Del Mar, C.B. Doctors do not adequately look after their own physical health. Med J Aust 2004; 181: 368–370.

6 Good medical practice: a code of conduct for doctors in Australia https://www.medicalboard.gov.au/Codes-Guidelines-Policies.aspx.

7 Elton C. Also human: The inner lives of doctors. William Heinemann, London, 2018.

8 Vaillant G E, Sobowale N C, McArthur C. Some psychologic vulnerabilities of physicians. New Engl J Med 1972: 287; 372–5.

9 Klitzman R. When doctors become patients. Oxford University Press 2008. Although based on the stories of US doctors, this book emphasises how doctors with serious illness can jeopardise their own care by seeking to be both patient and doctor.

10 Elton C. Also human: The inner lives of doctors. William Heinemann, London, 2018.

11 Physicians with Health Conditions: Law and Policy Reform to Protect the Public and Physician-Patients. Report of the Health Law Institute, Alberta, Canada 2012.

12 Kay M, Mitchell G, Clavarino A et al. Doctors as patients: A systematic review of doctors' health access and the barriers they experience. British Journal of General Practice 2008; 58: 501–508.

13 Jena AB et al. Why physicians work when sick. Archives of Internal Medicine 2012; 172(14): 1107–1108.

14 Presenteeism, invented as a term opposite to absenteeism, refers here to working when unwell.

15 https://www.medscape.com/viewarticle/983480?src=wnl_tp10_daily_221106_MSCPEDIT&uac=284664HX&impID=48308.

16 https://www.drs4drs.com.au/help-another-doctor/.

17 Tyssen R. Health problems and the use of health services among physicians: A review article with particular emphasis on Norwegian Studies. Industrial Health. 2007, 45; 599–610.

Chapter 8

1 Quek TC, Wai-San W, Tran BX et al. One in three medical students suffer anxiety, a prevalence rate much higher than in the general population. The Global Prevalence of Anxiety Among Medical Students: A Meta-Analysis. Int J Environ Res Public Health 2019; 16(15): 2735.

2 As mentioned in Chapter 10, about one third of the case load at the Victorian Doctors' Health Program consists of distressed medical students and one third junior doctors.

3 Markwell AL, Wainer Z. The health and wellbeing of junior doctors: insights from a national survey. Med J Aust 2009; 191 (8): 441–444.

4 https://medicine.uq.edu.au/files/42088/Beyondblue%20Doctors%20Mental%20health.pdf.

5 Bailey E, Robinson J, McGorry P. Depression and suicide among medical practitioners in Australia. Internal Medicine Journal 2018; 48: 254–258.

6 Dyrbye LN, Thomas MR, Shanafelt TD. Systematic review of depression, anxiety, and other indicators of psychological distress among U.S. and Canadian medical students. Academic Medicine 2006; 81(4): 354–373. https://journals.lww.com/academicmedicine/Fulltext/2006/04000/Decreasing_GME_Training_Stress_to_Foster.00009.aspx.

7 A meta-analysis refers to a systematic review of existing research findings.

8 https://www.ncbi.nlm.nih.gov/pmc/articles/PMC6509028/.

9 https://pubmed.ncbi.nlm.nih.gov/31604726/.

10 Throughout this book the term 'junior doctor' covers all doctors from the point of graduation through their entire training which may extend to eight or more years.

11 Reynolds CF. Preventing suicidal ideation in medical interns. JAMA Psychiatry 2015; 72(12): 1169.

12 Guille C et al. Web-based cognitive behavioural therapy intervention for the prevention of suicidal ideation in medical interns: A randomized clinical trial. JAMA Psychiatry 2015; 72(12): 1192–98.

13 There has been considerable research conducted in the UK as to why young people seek to become doctors. The best designed study identified four main driving forces: a desire to help others; a need to be indispensable; a wish to be a scientist; and a wish to be respected by society. McManus IC, Livingston G, Katona C. The attractions of medicine: the generic motivations of medical school applicants in relation to demography, personality and achievement. BMC Education, 2006, 6: 11.

14 Gerada C. Beneath the White Coat: Doctors, Their Minds and Mental Health. Routledge, 2021, p 41.

15 A literature search failed to find data on the mental health of OTDs. Even the searching examination of the issues faced by OTDs conducted by a Federal Parliamentary Committee did not comment on this matter. Lost in the Labyrinth: Report on the inquiry into registration processes and support for overseas trained doctors. House of Representatives Standing Committee on Health and Ageing, March 2012.

16 Physicians with Health Conditions: Law and Policy Reform to Protect the Public and Physician-Patients. Report of the Health Law Institute, Alberta, Canada 2012.

17 Epstein RM, Privitera MR. Comment. Addressing physician mental health. Lancet Psychiatry, 2019; 6(3): 190–191.

18 Average hours worked by junior doctors are still long at around 55–57 hours per week. Many work even longer than that average with one study reporting that 25% worked 65 hours per week. Axisa C, Nash L, Kelly P, Willcock S. Psychiatric morbidity, burnout and distress in Australian physician trainees. Aust Health Rev. 2020; 44(1): 31–38.

19 The 2021 survey of doctors in training conducted by the Medical Board of Australia found that 16% of doctors were never paid for overtime and another 23% were paid sometimes. https://medicaltrainingsurvey.gov.au/.

20 In Victoria in 2021, 47% of junior doctors reported unpaid overtime and a group of junior doctors were planning a class action over this. https://www.abc.net.au/news/2021-05-19/junior-doctors-new-class-action-claiming-unpaid-overtime/100147606.

21 Medical Board of Australia 'Medical training survey' 2022. https://www.medicaltrainingsurvey.gov.au/Results/Reports-and-results.

22 Nash LM, Daly MG, Kelly PJ, et al. Factors associated with psychiatric morbidity and hazardous alcohol use in Australian doctors. Med J Aust 2010; 193(3): 161–166.

23 In the 2021 survey of junior doctors conducted by the Medical Board of Australia it was reported that 'bullying, harassment, discrimination and racism' was experienced by 34%, a figure that had not improved since the surveys began. https://medicaltrainingsurvey.gov.au/.

24 Haysom, G. The impact of complaints on doctors. Australian Family Physician 2016; 45(4): 242–244.

25 https://www.safetyandquality.gov.au/sites/default/files/migrated/Australian-Open-Disclosure-Framework-Feb-2014.pdf.

26 Bradfield OM et al. Medical negligence claims and the health and life satisfaction of Australian doctors: a prospective cohort analysis of the MABEL survey. BMJ Open 2022; 12(5): e059447.

27 https://www.smh.com.au/opinion/three-of-my-colleagues-have-killed-themselves-medicines-dark-secret-cant-be-allowed-to-go-on-20170209-gu9crd.html.

28 Breen K J. So you want to be a doctor. Australian Scholarly Publishing 2nd ed, 2020, pp 98–105.

29 Ibid. pp 118–123.

30 Petrie K, Crawford J, LaMontagne AD, et al. Working hours, common mental disorder and suicidal ideation among junior doctors in Australia: a cross-sectional survey. BMJ Open 2020; 10: e033525. Junior doctors working more than 55 hours a week (a quarter of the cohort) reported a doubling of mental health issues and suicidal ideation.

31 Axisa C, Nash L, Kelly P, Willcock S. Psychiatric morbidity, burnout and distress in Australian physician trainees. Aust Health Rev 2020; 44(1): 31–38.

32 Elton C. Also human: The inner lives of doctors. William Heinemann, London, 2018.

33 McCranie EW, Brandsma JM. Personality antecedents of burnout among middle-aged physicians. Behavioral Medicine 1988; 14: 30–36.

34 Dyrbye L, Shanafelt T. A narrative review on burnout experienced by medical students and residents. Med Educ 2016; 50(1): 132–49.

35 Gerada C. Beneath the White Coat: Doctors, Their Minds and Mental Health. Routledge, 2021, p 86.

36 https://www.ausdoc.com.au/news/three-minutes-per-patient-doctors-outraged-over-hospital-management-directive/.

37 Hornsby Ku-ring-gai Hospital apologises to junior doctors after threatening to make it harder to rest on late shifts – ABC News.

38 Breen K J. So you want to be a doctor. Australian Scholarly Publishing 2nd ed, 2020, p 102.

39 https://www.ncis.org.au/research-and-publications/ncis-fact-sheets/intentional-self-harm-health-professionals/.

40 Bailey E, Robinson J and McGorry P. Depression and suicide among medical practitioners in Australia. Internal Medicine Journal, 2018; 48: 254–258.

41 Goldney R D. Suicide by health care professionals. Medical Journal of Australia, 2016; 205 (6): 257–258.

42 https://www.saxinstitute.org.au/publications/evidence-check-library/suicide-prevention-in-high-risk-occupations/.

43 https://www.gmc-uk.org/-/media/documents/doctors-who-have-died-while-under-investigation-or-during-a-period-of-monitoring-2018-2020--89398370.pdf.

44 Australian and New Zealand doctors' experiences of disciplinary notifications,

investigations, proceedings and interventions relating to alleged mental health impairment: a qualitative analysis of interviews. Bradfield O, et al. International Journal of Law and Psychiatry, 2023; 86: 101857.

45 Robinson N. The race to save the doctors who are dying of 'shame'. The Australian, March 25, 2023.

46 Australian and New Zealand doctors' experiences of disciplinary notifications, investigations, proceedings and interventions relating to alleged mental health impairment: a qualitative analysis of interviews. Bradfield O, et al. International Journal of Law and Psychiatry, 2023; 86: 101857.

Chapter 9

1 Opioid drugs include morphine, codeine, oxycodone, pethidine, fentanyl and heroin. Heroin is now an illegal drug but in the distant past it was widely prescribed by doctors.

2 Benzodiazepines include a range of long-acting and shorter acting drugs of which the best know is diazepam (Valium). They are all addictive and withdrawal is a problem after prolonged use. They can be hazardous when combined with excessive alcohol intake.

3 Cadman M, Bell J. Doctors detected self-administering opioids in New South Wales, 1985–1994: characteristics and outcomes. Med J Aust 1998; 169: 419–421.

4 Oreskovich M R et al. The Prevalence of Substance Use Disorders in American Physicians. American Journal of Addiction 2015; 24(1): 30–38. A recent USA study reported that 13% of male physicians and 21% of female physicians met diagnostic criteria for alcohol abuse or dependence.

5 Wilson J et al. Characterization of Problematic Alcohol Use Among Physicians: A Systematic Review. JAMA Open2022; 5(12): e2244679.

6 Nash LM, Daly MG, Kelly PJ, et al. Factors associated with psychiatric morbidity and hazardous alcohol use in Australian doctors. Med J Aust 2010; 193(3): 161–166.

7 Pilgrim JL, Dorward R and Drummer OH. Drug-caused deaths in Australian medical practitioners and health-care professionals. Addiction 2016; 112: 486–491.

8 Twenty-two percent of Victorian doctors and medical students being treated for substance-abuse were addicted to illicit drugs. Wile C, Frei M, Jenkins K. Doctors and medical students case managed by an Australian doctors health program: Characteristics and outcomes. Australasian Psychiatry 2011; 19(3): 202–205.

9 Pilgrim JL, Dorward R, Drummer OH. Drug-caused deaths in Australian medical practitioners and health-care professionals. Addiction 2016; 112: 486–491.

10 Wile C, Jenkins K. The value of a support group for doctors with substance use disorders. Med J Aust 2012; 197(5): 275–6.

11 Breen KJ and Court JM. Doctors who self-administer drugs of dependence. Med J Aust 1998; 169 (8): 404–5.

12 Ibid.

Chapter 10

1 The term 'Australian health regulators' in this context refers to the Australian Health Practitioner Regulation Agency and the Medical Board of Australia. The two organisations describe themselves as the co-regulators of the medical profession and it is not always clear where responsibilities lie.

2 https://vdhp.org.au/ A more detailed description of VDHP is available in my book, Memoir of an accidental ethicist. Australian Scholarly Publishing, 2018, pp 79–100.

3 Gerada C. Beneath the White Coat: Doctors, Their Minds and Mental Health. Routledge, 2021, p 194.

4 Wile C, Frei M, Jenkins K. Doctors and Medical Students Case Managed by an Australian Doctors Health Program: Characteristics and Outcomes. Australasian Psychiatry 2011; 19(3): 202–205.

5 I have my doubts about those intentions as I suspect that deep down the intentions included once and for all destroying the concept that the medical profession was self-regulating.

6 Brooke D. Impairment in the medical and legal professions. Journal of Psychosomatic Research, 1997; 43, 27–34.

7 https://www.drs4drs.com.au/.

8 Physicians with Health Conditions: Law and Policy Reform to Protect the Public and Physician-Patients. Report of the Health Law Institute, Alberta, Canada 2012.

9 Some of the doctors' health programs in the USA have been the subject of criticism. See Lenzer J. Physician health programs under fire. BMJ 2016; 353: i3568.

10 My long-held views on this aspect are supported by the conclusions of a recent Australian study of the experience of unwell doctors in the hands of the national regulator. See Bradfield OM et al. Medical negligence claims and the health and life satisfaction of Australian doctors: a prospective cohort analysis of the MABEL survey. BMJ Open 2022; 12(5): e059447.

11 For a helpful discussion of the notion of a social contract, see https://journalofethics.ama-assn.org/article/physician-health-programs-and-social-contract/2016-01.

Chapter 11

1 https://insightplus.mja.com.au/2019/5/mandatory-reporting-regulatory-bullying-racgp-president/?utm_source=InSight%252B&utm_campaign=9f5fa35322-EMAIL_CAMPAIGN_2019_02_08_05_10&utm_medium=email&utm_term=0_7346f35e23-9f5fa35322-42153349.

2 Breen K J. National registration legislative proposals need more work and more time. Med J Aust 2009; 191: 464–465.

3 The same issue seems to exist in the UK as the editor of a book published in 2016 observed that 'the idea of linking health issues with professional misconduct issues in one system seems to me to take us back to stigma and is unhelpful'. Doctors as patients. P Jones (Ed). 2005, CRC Press, Taylor& Francis Group.

4   Not only did the law use the past tense but no guidance was provided as to how far back in time was 'past'. The law was amended several years later.

5   https://blogs.bmj.com/bmj/2019/06/10/australias-health-ministers-ignore-concerns-about-mandatory-reporting-of-unwell-doctors/.

6   Guidelines: Mandatory notifications about registered health practitioners. https://www.medicalboard.gov.au/Codes-Guidelines-Policies.aspx.

7   In defence of AHPRA, after 12 years of operating, it has belatedly brought in part-time clinical advisors to support its non-clinically trained investigative staff. See discussion in Bradfield OM et al. Medical negligence claims and the health and life satisfaction of Australian doctors: a prospective cohort analysis of the MABEL survey. BMJ Open 2022; 12 (5): e059447.

8   During the writing of this book, a new Australian study was published confirming that fear of the regulator is a major factor that leads to delays in doctors seeking help. Bradfield O. et al. Australian and New Zealand doctors' experiences of disciplinary notifications, investigations, proceedings and interventions relating to alleged mental health impairment: a qualitative analysis of interviews. International Journal of Law and Psychiatry 2023; 86: 101857.

9   For insight into how practising doctors struggle with understanding and fulfilling the mandatory reporting requirements see Bismark MM et al. Views on mandatory reporting of impaired health practitioners by their treating practitioners: a qualitative study from Australia. BMJ Open 2016; 6(12): e011988.

10 http://johnmenadue.com/?p=10190.

Chapter 12

1   https://www.bitre.gov.au/statistics/safety/fatal_road_crash_database.

2   The first three months of internship in the hospital in which any new doctor undertook most of her/his training can be stressful but it is much more stressful to spend these first months in an unfamiliar hospital.

3   https://www.theguardian.com/money/2014/sep/01/surgeons-doctors-cause-most-accidents-insurance.

4   Under the European Working Time Directive issued in 2000, the maximum hours of work are set at 48 hours per week while in the USA, since 2011 the maximum work week for junior doctors is 80 hours.

5   Barger LK, Cade BE, Ayas NT et al. Extended work hours and the risk of motor vehicle crashes among interns. New Engl J Med 2005; 352: 125–134.

6   Ibid.

7   Cai, A.W.T., Manousakis, J.E., Singh, B. et al. On-road driving impairment following sleep deprivation differs according to age. Sci Rep 2021; 11: 21561.

8   Sprajcer M, Dawson D, Kosmadopoulos A, et al. How tired is too tired to drive? A systematic review assessing the use of prior sleep duration to detect driving impairment. Nature and Science of Sleep 2023; 15: 175–206.

9   No longer called 'interns' in Australia but are commonly referred to as 'hospital medical officers, year one' (HMO1).

10 https://ama.com.au/sites/default/files/documents/150717%20-%20AMA%20
Safe%20Hours%20Audit%202016.pdf.

11 The 2021 survey of doctors in training conducted by the Medical Board of
Australia revealed that 12% of doctors had worked more the 60 hours per week
and 2% more than 90 hours. https://medicaltrainingsurvey.gov.au/.

12 Petrie K, Crawford J, LaMontagne AD, et al. Working hours, common mental
disorder and suicidal ideation among junior doctors in Australia: a cross-sectional
survey. BMJ Open 2020; 10: e033525. https://bmjopen.bmj.com/content/10/1/
e033525.

13 Axisa C. et al. Psychiatric morbidity, burnout and distress in Australian physician
trainees. Australian Health Review 2020: 44(1); 31–38.

14 https://www.sleepfoundation.org/excessive-sleepiness/workplace-accidents.

15 Landrigan CP, Rothschild JM, Cronin JW, et al. Effect of reducing interns' work
hours on serious medical errors in intensive care units. N Engl J Med 2004; 351:
1838–1848.

16 Lockley SW, Cronin JW, Evans EE, et al. Effect of reducing interns' weekly work
hours on sleep and attentional failures. N Engl J Med 2004; 351: 1829–37.

17 Grantcharov TP, Bardram L, Funch-Jensen P, Rosenberg J. Laparoscopic
performance after one night on call in a surgical department: prospective study.
BMJ 2001; 323: 1222–3.

18 Eastridge BJ, Hamilton EC, O'Keefe GE, et al. Effect of sleep deprivation on
the performance of simulated laparoscopic surgical skill. Am J Surg 2003; 186:
169–74.

Chapter 13

1 White GE. Sexual harassment during medical training: the perception of medical
students at a university medical school in Australia. Medical Education 2000; 34:
980–6.

2 Wilkinson TJ, Gill DJ, Fitzjohn J et al. The impact on students of adverse
experiences during medical education. Medical Teacher 2006: 28; 129–135.

3 Abate L E and Greenberg L. Incivility in medical education: a scoping review.
BMC Medical Education. 2023 Jan 12; 23(1): 24.

4 Crombie KE, Crombie KD, Salie M and Seedat S. Medical Students' Experiences
of Mistreatment by Clinicians and Academics at a South African University.
Teach Learn Med. 2023; Jan 17; 1–10.

5 Cook DJ, Liutkus JF, Risdon CL et al. Residents' experiences of abuse,
discrimination and sexual harassment during residency training. Can Med Assoc
Journal 1996; 154(11): 1657–65.

6 Fnais N. et al. Harassment and discrimination in medical training: a systematic
review and meta-analysis. Academic Medicine. 2014; May 89(5): 817–27.

7 https://medicaltrainingsurvey.gov.au/.

8 https://www.medicaltrainingsurvey.gov.au/Results/Reports-and-results.

9 https://www.abc.net.au/news/2015-03-09/gabrielle-mcmullin-stands-by-sexual-
harassment-comments/6292066.

10 https://www.surgeons.org/-/media/Project/RACS/surgeons-org/files/BR-Eval-Report-FINAL-2021-11-03.pdf?rev=e4ddd607de944024aa91cac297e1a80e&hash=ECF21DA58179792C1581B6821D1F2CE5.

11 Vasey C E et al. Navigating parenthood in the surgical profession: mixed-methods study. British Journal of Surgery 2023, 110, 84–91.

12 Kirby M. Patient's rights – why the Australian courts have rejected 'Bolam'. Journal of Medical Ethics 1995; 21: 5–8.

13 Breen KJ, Weisbrot D. A no-fault compensation system for medical injury is long overdue. Med J Aust 2012: 197; 296–298.

14 Robinson N. The race to save the doctors who are dying of 'shame'. *The Australian*, March 25, 2023.

15 https://johnmenadue.com/a-matter-of-conscience-what-to-do-about-the-national-medical-regulator/.

Chapter 14

1 Gerada C. Beneath the White Coat: Doctors, Their Minds and Mental Health. Routledge, 2021, p 61.

2 My view that systems need to change and not the responses of doctors is supported by this recent thoughtful essay: Arnold-Forster A, Moses JD, Schotland SV. Obstacles to Physicians' Emotional Health – Lessons from History. N Engl J Med 2022; 386(1): 4–7.

3 Glozier N. Distress and career regret in doctors: are we really that different to other professions? Med J Aust 2023; 218(6): 254–255.

4 Some medical schools explicitly advise the need for a driver's licence and provision of one's own means of transport.

5 Garrud P, McManus IC. Impact of accelerated, graduate-entry medicine courses: a comparison of profile, success, and specialty destination between graduate entrants to accelerated or standard medicine courses in UK. BMC Medical Education 2018; 18(1): 250.

6 The inquiry known as the 'Doherty Inquiry' reported in 1988. Its formal title was *Australian medical education and workforce into the 21st century*. Committee of Inquiry into Medical Education and Medical Workforce, Canberra: AGPS.

7 Teoh K, Singh J, Medisauskaite A, Hassard J. Doctors' perceived working conditions, psychological health and patient care: a meta-analysis of longitudinal studies. Occupational and Environmental Medicine 2023; 80(2): 61–69.

8 Glozier N. Distress and career regret in doctors: are we really that different to other professions? Med J Aust 2023; 218(6): 254–255.

9 It is not just doctors whose lives are at risk as medical students despatched to rural placements are also at risk.

10 But paid for fewer hours unless overtime is successfully claimed.

11 Petrie K, Crawford J, LaMontagne AD, et al. Working hours, common mental disorder and suicidal ideation among junior doctors in Australia: a cross-sectional survey. BMJ Open 2020; 10: e033525.

12 Ibid.

13 Rapid rotations between day and night shifts are highly undesirable and this will need to be kept in mind in any re-structuring.

14 In Victoria in the 1990s, where every local medical graduate was guaranteed a pre-registration intern year, a surfeit of new graduates led to major hospitals employing more interns than they really needed.

15 https://blogs.bmj.com/bmj/2019/06/10/australias-health-ministers-ignore-concerns-about-mandatory-reporting-of-unwell-doctors/.

16 Mainstreaming led to the closure of specialised psychiatric hospitals, the expansion of psychiatric wards in our public hospitals, and theoretically to enhanced care within the community.

17 Rowe L, Kidd MR. Increasing violence in Australian general practice is a public health issue. Med J Aust 2007; 187 (2): 118–119.

18 NSW has increased the maximum gaol sentence for people found guilty of assaulting front-line healthcare workers. Surprisingly general practitioners were not included in the definition of 'front-line healthcare worker'.

19 Ideally this should involve obtaining expert advice but at present such advice may not exist.

20 https://www.ncbi.nlm.nih.gov/pmc/articles/PMC3371777/.

21 https://www.audit.vic.gov.au/report/occupational-violence-against-healthcare-workers?section=32521--2-understanding-prevalence-and-severity&show-sections=1#32521--2-understanding-prevalence-and-severity.

22 Some reforms to medical indemnity insurance have reduced these stresses but have not removed them altogether. See Bradfield OM et al. Medical negligence claims and the health and life satisfaction of Australian doctors: a prospective cohort analysis of the MABEL survey. BMJ Open 2022; 12: e059447.

23 https://theconversation.com/why-dont-we-create-a-no-fault-scheme-for-medical-injuries-25329.

24 The national regulatory scheme is based on what is called the 'national law' which can be found here: http://classic.austlii.edu.au/au/legis/qld/consol_act/hprnl509/. It is not a national law but a template for the parliament of each state and territory to adopt as each chooses.

25 See for example Breen KJ. National registration legislative proposals need more work and more time. K J Breen. Med J Aust 191: 464–465; 2009; Breen KJ. Doctors' health: Can we do better under national registration? Med J Aust 2011: 194; 191–192; Breen KJ. National registration scheme at five years: not what it promised. Breen KJ. *Australian Health Review*, 2016; 40(6): 674–678.; and Breen KJ. What ails the national registration scheme for Australia's 600,000 health professionals? http://johnmenadue.com/blog/?p=6150 (11 April 2016).

26 The Medical Practitioners Board at that time was composed of twelve people: nine medical practitioners, two community members and a legally qualified member.

27 Mr Kim Snowball was engaged by the health ministers to review the national scheme. After consulting widely, he advised the ministers that they should copy the WA legislation and remove the mandatory requirement of reporting of unwell doctors by treating doctors.

28 Bradfield O. et al. Australian and New Zealand doctors' experiences of disciplinary notifications, investigations, proceedings and interventions relating to alleged mental health impairment: a qualitative analysis of interviews. International Journal of Law and Psychiatry, 2023; 86: 101857. This study strongly supports the concept of doctors' health programs, even though the report fails to mention the existence of such a program in Victoria since 2000.

29 Should the reader be interested in the complexity of the current Australian framework for the regulation of health professionals this article should be perused: Bennett B et al. Australia's National Registration and Accreditation Scheme for Health Practitioners: A National Approach to Polycentric Regulation? Sydney Law Review 2018; 40 (2): 159–181. I found it of additional interest as it confirmed my belief that there has been a determined push to diminish the central role of health professionals in their own regulation. Sadly the authors are blind to the negative impact of this push. Imagine the outcry should self-regulation be denied to lawyers!

30 Belatedly, after 12 years, AHPRA has come to appreciate that respect for the health professionals it regulates might repair the disrespect that most doctors have for the regulator. See Biggar S et al. Finding space for kindness: public protection and health professional regulation. International Journal for Quality in Health Care 2022; 34(3): mzac057.

31 In the 2022 book titled Doctors as Patients that he co-ordinated and edited, Dr Petre Jones expressed the view that 'the idea of linking health issues with professional misconduct issues in one system seems to me to take us back to stigma and is unhelpful'.

32 Bradfield O, Spittal M and Bismark M. Regulation in Need of Therapy? Analysis of Regulatory Decisions Relating to Impaired Doctors from 2010 to 2020: I. Introduction. Journal of Law and Medicine 2022; 29(4): 1090–1108.

33 Robinson R. The race to save the doctors who are dying of 'shame'. The Australian, March 25, 2023.

34 I have seen all the relevant correspondence in this case and can vouch for the accuracy of the doctor's account of what was a traumatic and totally unnecessary and unwarranted experience.

Epilogue

1 The AMA has pushed hard to improve the working hours of junior doctors and, via a recently issued statement, identified most of the desirable steps needed to improve the working conditions for junior and senior doctors in our public hospitals. See https://www.ama.com.au/articles/safe-healthy-and-supportive-work-environments-hospital-doctors-2023-position-statement.

2 Arnold-Forster A, Moses JD, Schotland SV. Obstacles to Physicians' Emotional Health – Lessons from History. N Engl J Med 2022; 386(1): 4–7.

Index

About the author

Dr Kerry Breen practised as a specialist physician in general internal medicine and gastroenterology at a major teaching hospital in Melbourne for most of his medical career. He was involved in teaching and examining medical students for the University of Melbourne and examining, on behalf of the Royal Australasian College of Physicians, junior doctors who were seeking to become specialist physicians. Mid-career he was appointed to the Medical Practitioners Board of Victoria on which he served for 19 years. He served as its president from 1994–2000 and there was instrumental in the establishment of the Victorian Doctors' Health Program. He has maintained a keen interest in the well-being of medical students and doctors and for five years served as the second chair of the Board of the Victorian Doctors' Health Program.

He also served as president of the Australian Medical Council during which time he oversaw the addition of an accreditation process for Australia's postgraduate medical colleges to the existing process of accreditation of Australia's medical schools. During the Australian Medical Council years he played a role in the development of the International Association of Medical Regulatory Authorities. He later served the National Health and Medical Research Council in a number of roles including chairmanship of its Australian Health Ethics Committee for two terms from 2000–2006. He currently holds an appointment as an Adjunct Professor at Monash

University via the Department of Forensic Medicine and the Victorian Institute of Forensic Medicine.

Early during his time on the Medical Practitioners Board of Victoria he recognised that the Board held an untapped repository of educational material for doctors and that many doctors who were otherwise competent had gaps in their knowledge and understanding of the everyday ethical and legal issues that commonly arise in medical practice. In response to those gaps, with colleagues, he co-authored the text book *Good Medical Practice: Professionalism, Ethics and Law* which saw its fourth edition in 2016. He is also the author of *So You Want To Be a Doctor: A Guide For Prospective and Current Medical Students in Australia*, now in its second edition.

Dr Breen supported the concept of national medical registration but has been deeply disappointed with the structure, implementation, and lack of national coverage of the scheme that was hastily introduced in 2010. He has urged major reform to the scheme, so far without success.

This book reflects all of the above interests and experience, in particular his concern for the well-being of medical students and doctors. This concern is complemented by his appreciation of the delicate balance for medical regulators involved in ensuring the safety of patients while also supporting the well-being of the doctors who care for those patients.

Printed in Australia
Ingram Content Group Australia Pty Ltd
AUHW020854171024
401396AU00003B/79